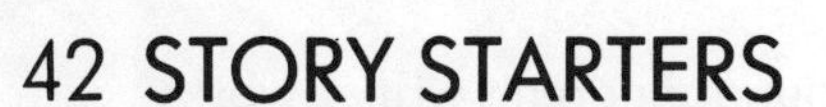

INTRODUCTION

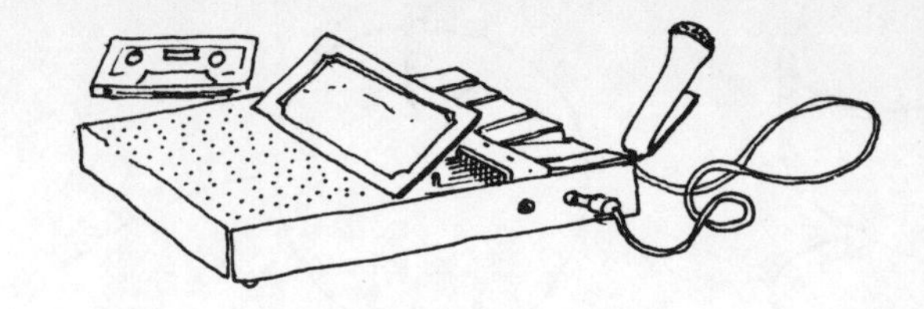

As teachers, one of our main concerns is to help children develop their spoken language skills. Not only will these skills be needed to underpin the later skills of reading and writing but, even more important, speech is still the way most of us communicate with each other most of the time.

The majority of children learn to speak long before they start school. The richness of their vocabulary and the skill with which they handle language will vary dramatically. Our job is to start where the children are and to go on to help them say what they want to say in a way which enables others to understand. They will need the basic tools of vocabulary and syntax, plus plenty of experiences which they want to talk about and the opportunities to do so.

This book sets out to help you provide these things. You can dip into it for quick ideas on activities and games to introduce and reinforce different aspects of language development work with children aged five to eleven years. You are not expected to work through each activity and section in turn, but to pull out whatever you need to back up current language classwork. The suggestions are tried and tested ideas based on material from Scholastic's magazines.

The activities are grouped into four main sections: Vocabulary Stretchers; Story Starters; Getting the Message Across; Rhymes, Riddles and Nonsense. Each section moves from simple to more complex language concepts. There is a mixture of small-/large-group and whole-class activities.

VOCABULARY STRETCHERS

Words are the basic tools of language. This section concentrates on activities for introducing and reinforcing a range of basic vocabulary from simple nouns to adjectives, adverbs, prepositions, prefixes and suffixes.

The early activities can be used to give children an opportunity to show whether or not they can recognize letter sounds and shapes and to reveal the range of their existing vocabulary. They may also highlight hearing and pronunciation difficulties. Other activities give children practice in using language to classify, order and compare properties both within and across categories. The later activities encourage children to pool their ideas to build up a communal vocabulary bank which they can draw on for creative story-telling.

STORY STARTERS

All too often young children's written work lacks the sparkle and variety of their speech – their imaginations are curtailed by the chore of getting the words down on paper. So the emphasis in this section is on telling (either directly or on tape) rather than writing stories. The activities are all based on providing a stimulus for story-telling, ranging from an exciting first sentence to miscellaneous objects which have to be woven into the story-line. The activities are also aimed at helping the children appreciate the way stories are structured – they may have to create a beginning, middle or end for a story, or rearrange an existing story so that it follows a logical sequence.

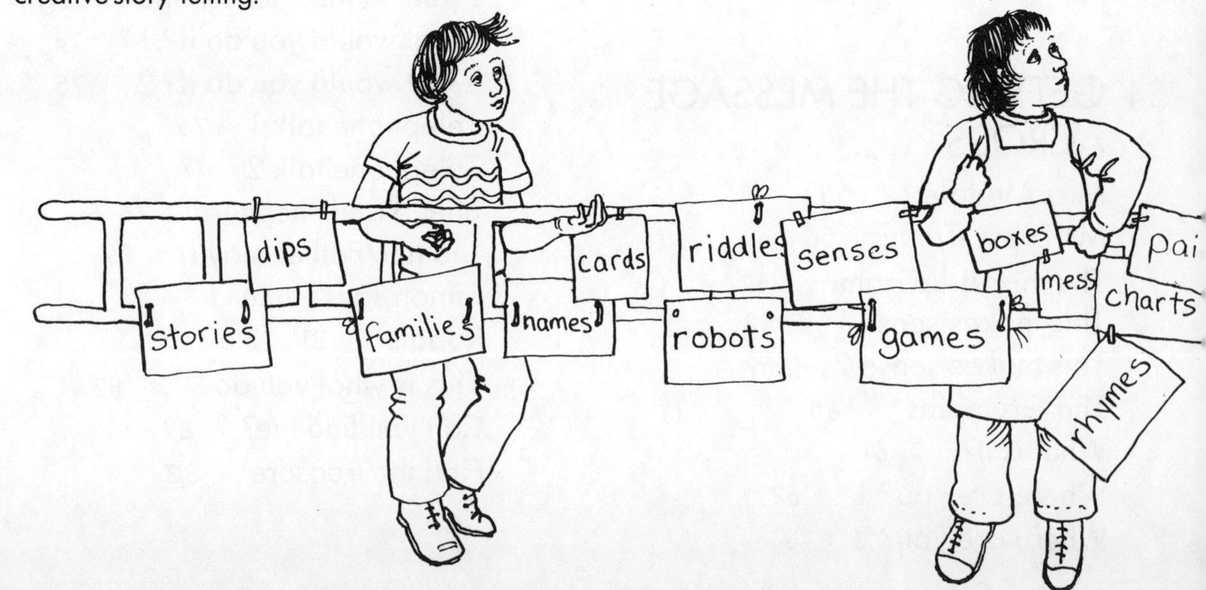

BRIGHT IDEAS FOR LANGUAGE DEVELOPMENT

from *Scholastic Magazines*

Ward Lock Educational/Scholastic

Published by Scholastic Publications (Magazines) Ltd and Ward Lock Educational Co Ltd.

Ward Lock Educational Co Ltd
47 Marylebone Lane London W1A 6AX
A Ling Kee Company

Scholastic Publications (Magazines) Ltd
9 Parade Leamington Spa
Warwickshire CV32 4DG

Ideas drawn from Scholastic's magazines, including *Child Education, Junior Education* and *Art and Craft*.

Compiled by Frankie Leibe
Edited by Sue Quilliam
Illustrated by Jane Bottomley

ISBN 0-7062-4452-4

Front and back covers: Liquid surface reacting to sound waves, Science Photo Library.

CONTENTS

GETTING THE MESSAGE ACROSS

This section concentrates on two aspects of spoken communication: the basic syntax and constructions we have to use to make what we say intelligible, and the need to select and organize information in order to present it effectively.

The earlier activities, which deal with basic syntax and constructions, will be particularly useful with children who are learning English as a second language. The constant practice and repetition needed to master these basics and fix them in the children's minds can be a chore; these activities aim to make them fun both for you and the children.

The later activities give practice in seeking and presenting different kinds of information in different situations for different audiences.

RHYMES, RIDDLES AND NONSENSE

Most children love to play with words – they enjoy jokes, riddles and puns, the cornier the better. This section capitalizes on that enjoyment to encourage children to listen, memorize and reproduce sound – all important aspects of using language. It begins with the children's own rhymes which they use as an integral part of their play, and moves on to activities which involve playing with words both for pure fun and as part of communicating meaning.

An essential part of any language work is practice. As mentioned earlier, we need to make sure that the children have something they really want to talk about and the opportunities to do so, both with each other and with adults. Perhaps, above all, we and the children need to remember that communication is a two-way process. There is little point in helping children to express themselves clearly and fluently unless we (and they) are prepared to listen to each other.

The illustrations on pages 108–123 can be used to make the cards needed for several of the activities. They can be cut out, stuck on to card or covered with clear film to prolong their life. The children may like to colour them first. Where several sets of cards are needed the pages may be photocopied.

Frankie Leibe

VOCABULARY STRETCHERS

Password

Age range
Five to seven.

Group size
Small group, ie five or six children.

What you need
A ball or a bean bag.

What to do
The children sit with you in a circle. You choose a topic (eg food), make the sound of a certain letter (eg *s*), and then hand the ball or bean bag to one of the children. He/she has to say a word beginning with that letter – sausage, for example – and then pass the ball to the next child who has to provide another food word beginning with *s*, and so on. Anyone who cannot think of an appropriate word can miss a go and pass the ball on to the next player. When all the children have run out of ideas, either choose another letter or another topic, eg toys, clothes, animals, scary things, nice things.

I went to market and I bought . . .

Age range
Five to nine.

Group size
Small group, ie five or six children.

What you need
No materials needed.

What to do
The children sit with you in a small circle. You either hold, show or give them a letter of the alphabet and the children take it in turns to think of things they might have bought beginning with that letter. So the first child would start off, 'I went to market and I bought an apple'. The next child would have to think of something else beginning with *a* – for example an apricot – and so on. Once every child has had a turn, a new letter is chosen and the game begins again.

The game can be made more difficult by asking each player to repeat the list of what other players bought, eg 'I went to market and I bought an apple, an apricot and an avocado pear'.

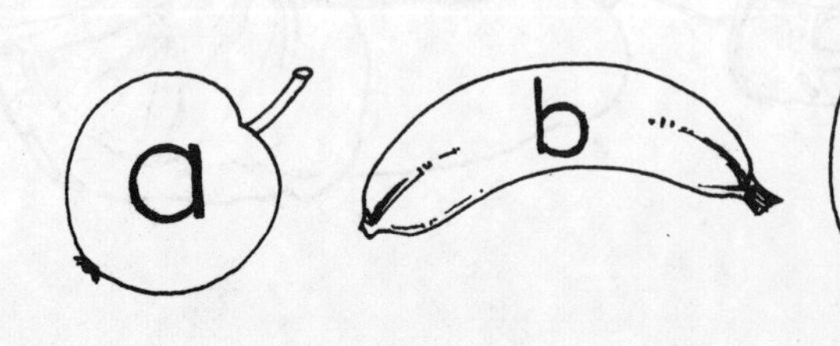

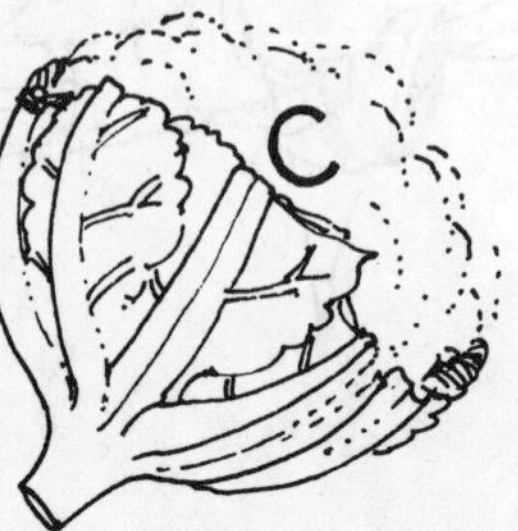

Letter games

Age range
Five to seven.

Group size
Small group, ie five or six children.

What you need
Alphabet fish, ie paper fish shapes, each with a different consonant written on it, to be caught with a string line and magnet.

What to do
Each child takes it in turn to catch a fish and then has to name objects starting with the letter shown on the fish. To make the game slightly more difficult the objects may have to be animals, food, clothes or verbs, adverbs, adjectives, etc.

Where do I belong?

Age range
Five to nine.

Group size
Whole class or large group.

What you need
Coloured pictures (photographs or drawings) of different food, clothing, animals, toys, tools, etc.

What to do
Choose eight children to act as Mr and Mrs Food, Mr and Mrs Clothes, Mr and Mrs Animals and Mr and Mrs Toys. They set up home in four different parts of the classroom. The rest of the children are each given a picture which they have to identify. They then have to go to the right house and knock on the door. Mr and Mrs Whoever ask, 'Who are you?', and each child answers, 'I'm a potato/pair of trousers/zebra/rocket ship, etc. Can I come in?' If the child has chosen the right category the occupants say, 'You're something we eat/wear/play with/an animal so you can come in'.

When all the children have found a suitable home, the proud parents can take it in turn to introduce themselves and their children.

Follow-up
After a preliminary discussion, the idea can be extended to make a shopping game. Different shopkeepers, suitably labelled, can be stationed around the room. Potential customers are given pictures and have to work out which shop to go to. (Pat Hutchins' *Don't Forget the Bacon* or John Burningham's *The Shopping Basket* are both good follow-ups or starters for this game.)

Alternatively, children can classify items which are mentioned in a favourite story. It's best to concentrate on one category at a time (eg food or clothes, but not both). The children could then make a poster headed, for example, 'Things to Eat in *The Shopping Basket*' or 'Things to Wear in *How Do I Put It On?*', and illustrate it.

Stop card game

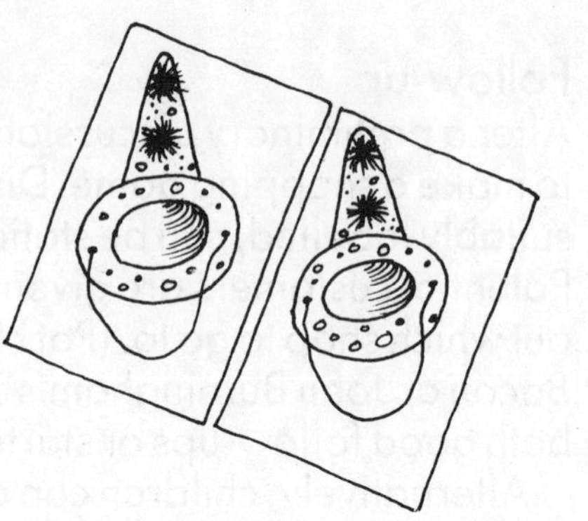

Age range
Five to nine.

Group size
Small group,
ie five to eight children.

What you need
A set of small cards (75×100 mm) showing pictures based on the vocabulary the class is currently working on, eg clothes, food, transport. There should be at least two cards of each object, and preferably three or four.

What to do
This is a variation on the game of Snap. The cards are dealt out among the players, who then take turns to place them face up on a central pile. As they do so they must give the name of the object, eg 'a boot', 'a scarf'. When two identical cards are placed on top of each other the first child to say, 'Stop. It's a shoe!' (or whatever) picks up the central pile.

Follow-up
The same cards can be used to play Bingo. Each child is dealt six or eight cards and lays them out, face up, like Bingo cards. You (or a helper or child) then hold up one card at a time, asking, 'Who's got a . . .?' The child who has the matching card calls out 'I have', and turns it face down. The first child to turn over all the cards is the winner and becomes the caller next time.

Pelmanism

Age range
Five to seven.

Group size
Small group, ie five to eight children.

What you need
A set of cards as described on page 10.

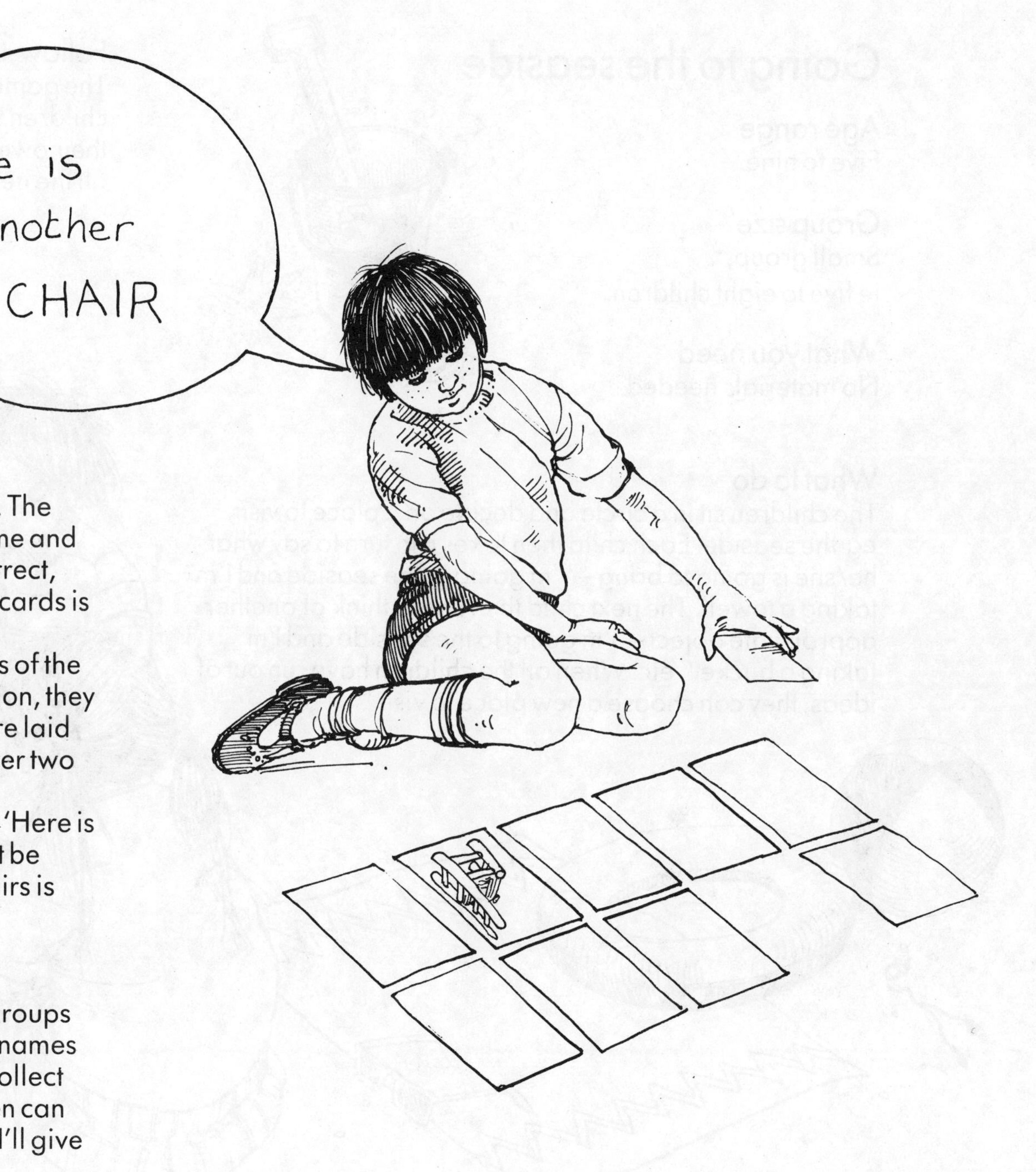

What to do
Spread out the cards face down on a desk or table. The children take it in turns to turn over one card at a time and say, 'It's a . . .'. If the name and the structure are correct, the child can keep the card. Whoever has the most cards is the winner.

When the children are confident about the names of the objects and have mastered the 'It's a . . .' construction, they might like to try real Pelmanism. Again the cards are laid out face down, but now the object is to try to turn over two identical cards (eg two tables or two chairs). The construction they will be using is 'Here is a . . .' and 'Here is another . . .'. If the two cards don't match, they must be turned face down again. The child with the most pairs is the winner.

Follow-up
More confident children could play a variation in groups of four. Each time a child turns over a card, he/she names the object – 'It's a . . .' – and keeps it. The aim is to collect sets of objects, eg sets of chairs, tables. The children can swap cards only by asking, 'If you give me a chair, I'll give you a table'.

Going to the seaside

Age range
Five to nine.

Group size
Small group,
ie five to eight children.

What you need
No materials needed.

What to do
The children sit in a circle and decide on a place to visit, eg the seaside. Each child then takes it in turn to say what he/she is going to bring – 'I'm going to the seaside and I'm taking a towel'. The next child then has to think of another appropriate object – 'I'm going to the seaside and I'm taking a bucket', etc. When all the children have run out of ideas, they can choose a new place to visit.

Follow-up
The game can be made more difficult by asking the children to repeat everyone else's item before adding their own or by giving a letter of the alphabet with which all the items have to begin.

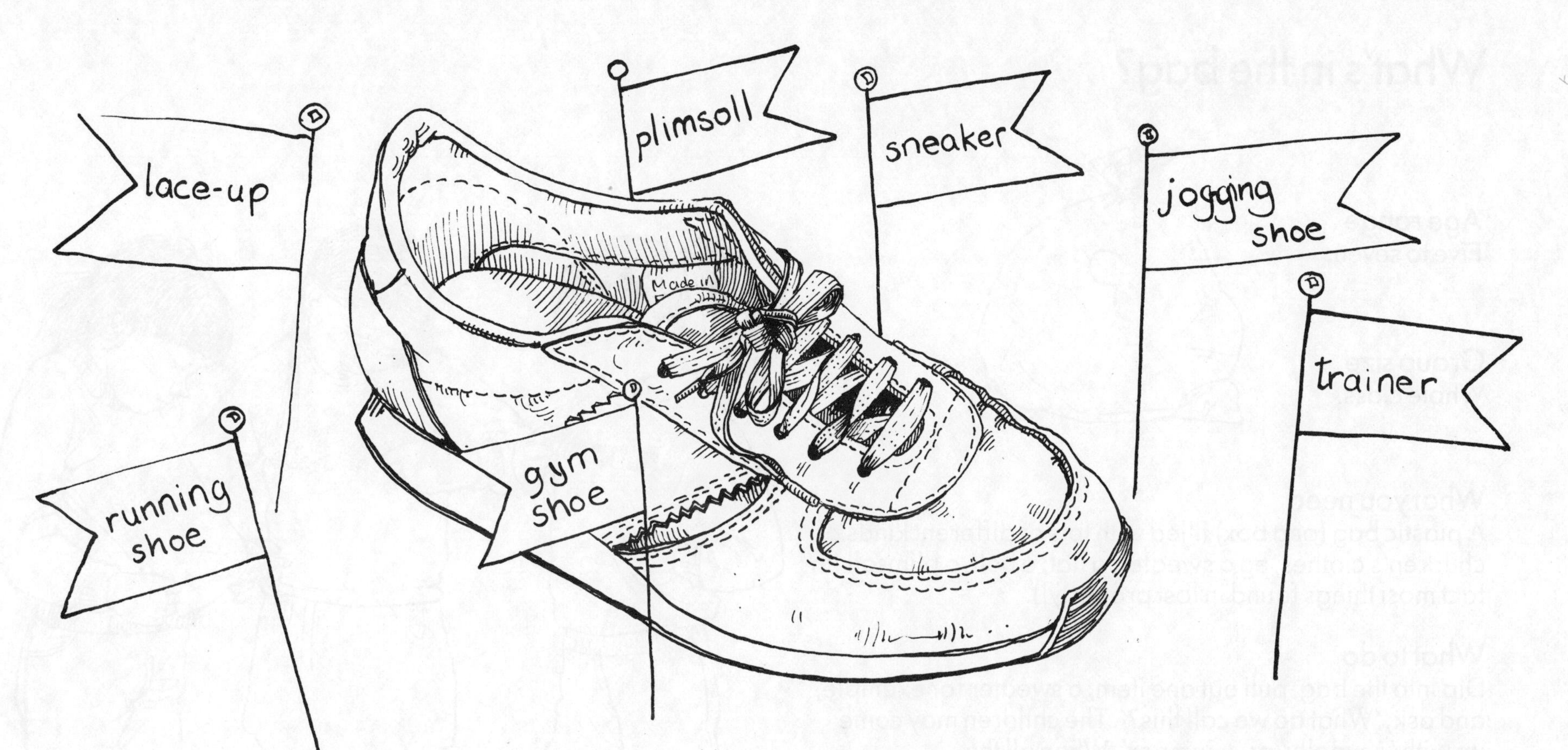

The name game

Age range
Five to nine.

Group size
Whole class.

What you need
Pictures of everyday objects, eg a car, a house, a shoe.

What to do
Show the class a picture of one of the objects and ask them to think of as many different names for it as they can. For example, a picture of a shoe might produce answers like sneaker, trainer, plimsoll, lace-up, running shoe.

The children may prefer to work in groups on a particular picture of something which really interests them. A group with a picture of a house might start with house or home, and with help move on to terraced house, two-storey house, etc. From there they can think of all the different types of homes people live in, ie flats, bungalows, chalets, cottages, castles, tents, etc, and draw or cut out pictures from magazines to illustrate their lists.

What's in the bag?

Age range
Five to seven.

Group size
Whole class.

What you need
A plastic bag (or a box) filled with lots of different kinds of children's clothes, eg a sweater, a hat, a belt, a plimsoll (in fact most things found in lost property!).

What to do
Dip into the bag, pull out one item, a sweater for example, and ask, 'What do we call this?'. The children may come up with 'A woolly' or 'A jumper'. When all the spontaneous replies have been exhausted, you can recap on all the suggestions and perhaps add others which haven't been mentioned, eg 'Well Jo calls it a woolly, and Jenny calls it a jumper. Another name for it is sweater'.

Follow-up
A variation on this theme which most children enjoy is finding the American equivalent of English words like sweets (candy), biscuits (cookies), pavement (sidewalk), lift (elevator), etc.

If yours is an area with a local dialect, the children could ask their parents or grandparents for their favourite dialect words.

Guess what it is

Age range
Seven to eleven.

Group size
Whole class.

What you need
As for 'What's in the bag?' (page 14).

What to do
One child is 'it' and has to cover or shut his/her eyes while another child reaches into the bag and pulls out one object. After the rest of the class have had a chance to see what it is, the object (a T-shirt for example) is put back into the bag and whoever is 'it' has to try to guess what the object was from the clues given by the rest of the class. The T-shirt might be described as follows:

It's cotton.
It's got short sleeves.
You can just pull it on – it hasn't got any buttons.
You wear it in the summer.

If the child who is 'it' guesses the right answer, he/she can choose a friend to be 'it' and the game continues.

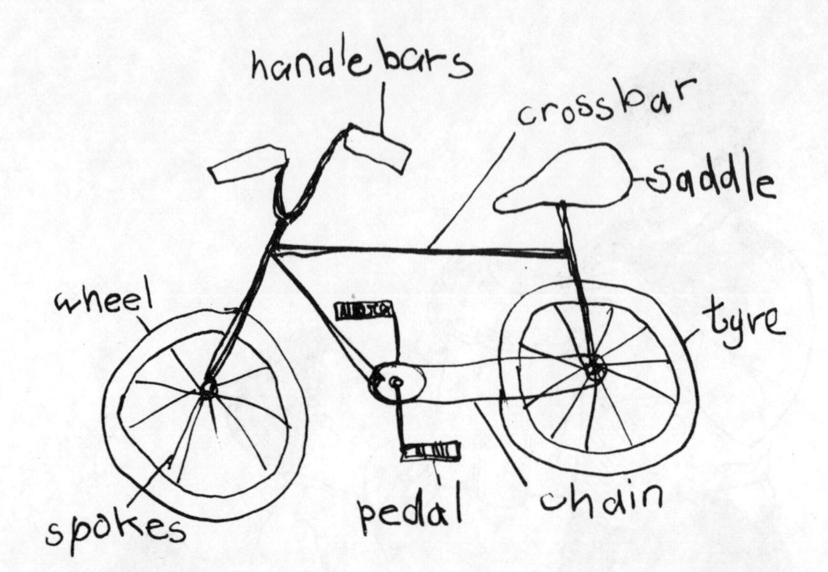

This is what it's called

Age range
Five to eleven.

Group size
Small group, ie five or six children.

What you need
Paper, glue, crayons.

What to do
Ask each child to find or draw a large picture of something which really interests him/her. It might be an animal, a bike, a car, a person, etc. He/she then dictates names for as many different parts of the object as he/she can think of. You write down the names and also help the child to think of names for other parts, or you can supply others which are missing. The child can then stick the labels on to the appropriate parts of the picture.

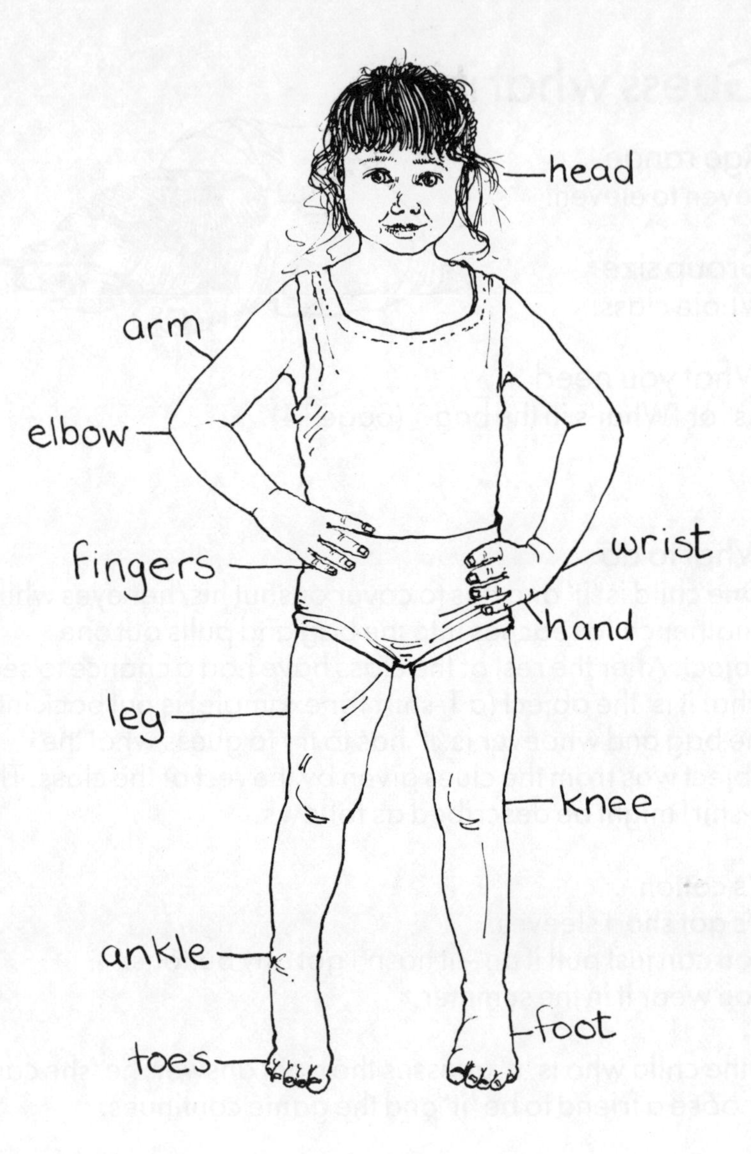

Follow-up
This activity could link in with the 'How many names?' game on page 18; the children could label the different parts of their bodies.

Who lives here?

Age range
Five to seven.

Group size
Whole class.

What you need
A House is a Home for Me by Mary Ann Hoberman.

What to do
After hearing the book read aloud and after general discussion about homes and houses, the children can try to supply the missing names for the animals which live in the following places:

A stable is a home for a . . . (horse/donkey).
A nest is a home for a . . . (bird).
A kennel is a home for a . . . (dog).
A pond is a home for a . . . (fish/newt/frog/tadpole).

The game can be made more open-ended by moving on to:

A sock is a home for a . . . (foot).
A shoe is a home for a . . . (foot).

or:

A dog is a home for a . . . (flea).

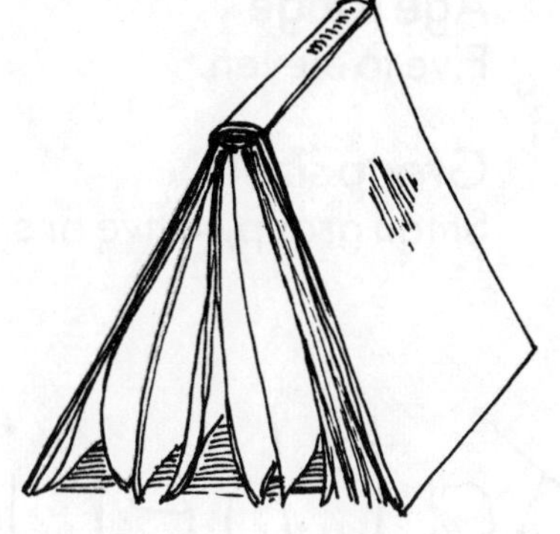

Follow-up
The children might like to use their imaginations to think of things which might live, for example, in a matchbox (other than matches), or an envelope (other than a letter), or a hole in the ground, etc.

How many names do I have?

Age range
Five to eleven.

Group size
Small group, ie five or six children.

Katherin

What you need
Any kind of drawing or painting materials and paper.

What to do
Ask the children to paint or draw a self-portrait and then to try to think of as many different names as possible to go with it. The obvious answers will be first names, surnames or nicknames, such as 'I am Jenny' or 'I am Delroy Richardson', but with help and general discussion the children will begin to see themselves in a wider family and social context and come up with suggestions like 'I am a girl', 'I am my father's eldest son', 'I am Nima's friend', 'I am Darren's sister', 'I am a ten-year-old', 'I am a pupil', etc. The children can write or dictate their labels and stick them on their portraits.

Follow-up
The children could use their portraits and labels as a basis for classification work, eg making sets of children with brothers or sisters, sets of only children, sets of youngest children.

Names 1

Age range
Five to seven.

Group size
Large group.

What you need
No materials needed.

What to do
Sit in a circle with the children. Turn to the child on your right and say, 'My name's Miss Morgan (or whatever), what's your name?'. The child then says, 'My name's Jemail, what's your name?', turning to the child on his right, and so on round the circle. Once all the children have given their names, ask them if anyone else in their family has that name – are they named after an aunt, or grandparent? Some children may have stories to tell about why they were given a particular name, eg it's the name of a film star, sports player, character from a book. Some of the children may know what their name means: Barry means spear, Deborah means bee. Find out if any of the children have nicknames – and again, why they were given them.

Follow-up
The children could make portraits of themselves, labelled with their names and/or nicknames, together with the meanings of their names. Older children could find out about surnames or how the months of the year and days of the week were given their names.

Names 2

Age range
Seven to eleven.

Group size
Whole class working in small groups.

What you need
No materials essential, but a couple of joke books and previously-prepared lists of funny names may be helpful.

What to do
Ask the children if they can tell you any book and author jokes, eg *Body in the Water* by Eileen Dover, *The Rich Man* by Ivor Million. Try giving groups authors and see if they can come up with suggestions for titles, eg Teresa Green, Justin Time, Ophelia Heart, Ann Tique, Enid Spankin, Miss L Toe. Some groups may come up with titles and authors – possibly even cover designs.

Some fictional names are deliberately chosen to tell us something about people. See if the class can guess what the following characters might be like: Augustus Gloop, Mike Teevee (from *Charlie and the Chocolate Factory*); Professor Branestawm, Mrs Flittersnoop, Colonel Dedshott, General Shatterfortz (from *Professor Branestawm and the Wild Letters*); Cacofonix, Marcus Ginantonicus (and many more – all from various *Asterix* books). Ask the groups to come up with ideas for names for characters like detectives, gardeners, misers, 'chinless wonders', etc.

Give each group a list of names like Sheila Sugar, Len Lemon, Hilda Honey, Terry Treacle, and ask them to invent a short sentence or phrase to describe how they would behave, eg 'I'd love to help you', said Sheila Sugar sweetly; Len Lemon smiled sourly; Terry Treacle gave a sickly smile; Victor Vinegar made an acid retort; 'Okay', said Simon Sparrow chirpily.

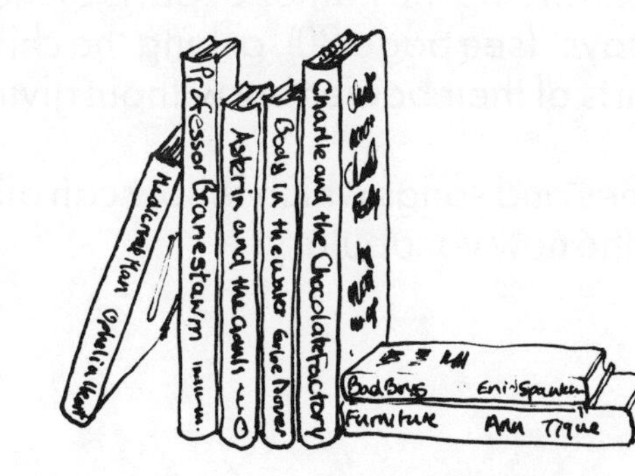

Those bones

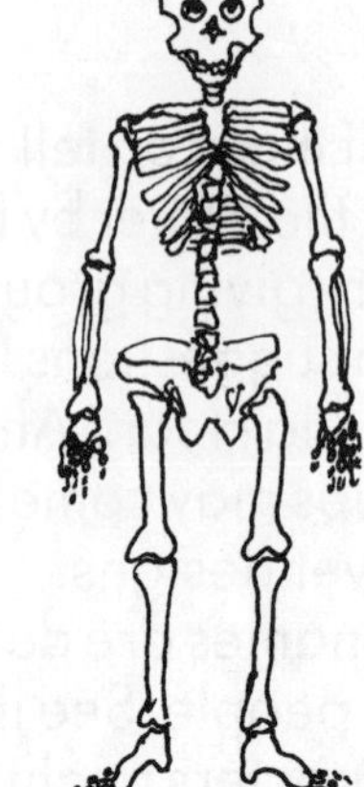

Age range
Five to nine.

Group size
Whole class.

What you need
No materials essential, but an Airfix skeleton will add zest.

What to do
By the time they come to school, most children know the names for the major parts of the body, but they can be a little hazy about wrists, ankles, etc. Teach the children the song, 'Those Bones', working carefully and systematically either up from the toes or down from the head so that all parts of the body are named. Once the children have learned the names, sing the song again, but leave gaps for individual children to fill in, eg 'The foot bone's connected to the . . .' (here you point at a child, who should supply 'ankle bone').

Follow-up
Another way of reinforcing the names of parts of the body is to play 'Simon says' (see page 80), asking the children to touch different parts of their bodies but without giving any action clues.

The action rhymes and songs which follow can all be used to reinforce the new vocabulary.

Heads and shoulders, knees and toes,
  knees and toes,
Heads and shoulders, knees and toes,
  knees and toes,
And eyes and ears and mouth and nose,
Heads and shoulders, knees and toes,
  knees and toes.
(Sung to the tune of 'There is a Tavern in the Town')

One finger, one thumb, keep moving,
One finger, one thumb, keep moving,
One finger, one thumb, keep moving,
We'll all be merry and bright.

One finger, one thumb, one arm, keep moving . . .
One finger, one thumb, one arm, one leg, keep moving . . .
One finger, one thumb, one arm, one leg, one nod of the head, keep moving . . .
One finger, one thumb, one arm, one leg, one nod of the head, stand up, sit down, keep moving . . .
One finger, one thumb, one arm, one leg, one nod of the head, stand up, sit down, turn round, keep moving . . .

Finger rhymes

Tommy Thumb, Tommy Thumb,
Where are you?
Here I am, here I am
How do you do?
Peter Pointer . . . (index finger),
Tommy Tall . . . (middle finger),
Ruby Ring . . . (ring finger),
Baby Small . . . (little finger).

Two fat gentlemen met in a lane (thumbs),
Bowed most politely, bowed once again.
How d'you do?
How d'you do?
How d'you do again?

Two thin ladies met in a lane . . . (index fingers),
Two tall policemen . . . (middle fingers),
Two young schoolboys . . . (ring fingers),
Two little babies . . . (little fingers).

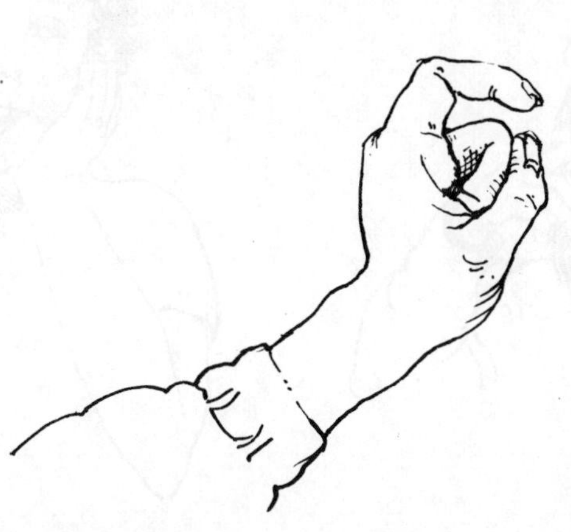

This is the way we do it

Age range
Five to nine.

Group size
Any size group.

What you need
No materials needed.

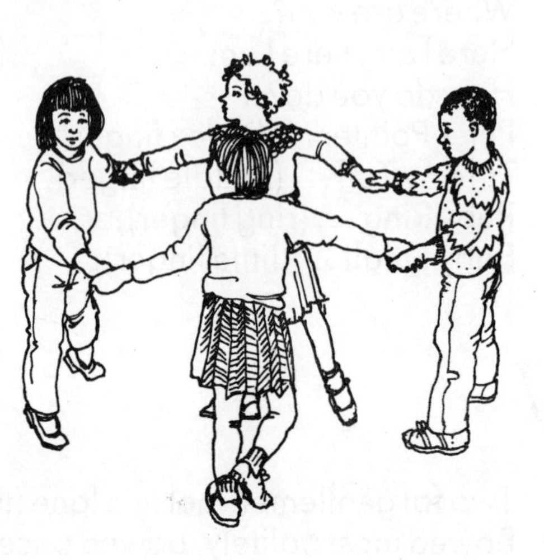

What to do
The traditional 'Here We Go Round the Mulberry Bush' tune can be adapted to help reinforce the names of parts of the body and the days of the week as the children sing and mime the following version:

This is the way we wash our hands,
Wash our hands, wash our hands,
This is the way we wash our hands,
Early on Monday morning.

This is the way we wash our faces,
. . . on Tuesday morning.

This is the way we clean our ears,
. . . on Wednesday morning.

This is the way we comb our hair,
. . . on Thursday morning.

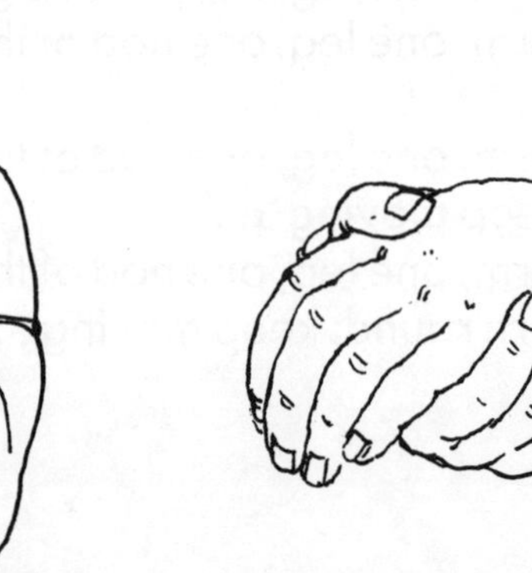

You can teach new verb forms by changing the subject, eg 'This is the way I wash/you wash/he or she washes/they wash'. Similarly the activities can be changed to simulate getting dressed – '. . . put on our coats/gloves/do up our shoes', etc.

Follow-up

Another useful song about the body, which also teaches left and right, is the 'Hokey Cokey'. Other suggestions are given on page 20.

This is the way we cut our nails,
. . . on Friday morning.

This is the way we blow our noses,
. . . on Saturday morning.

This is the way we wash our feet,
. . . on Sunday morning.

Whisk up a song

Age range
Five to seven.

Group size
Whole class.

What you need
A display of as many kitchen gadgets as possible: different types of whisk, grater, mincer, steamer, colander, sieve, potato peeler, tin opener, garlic press, pestle and mortar, etc.

What to do
Make a class display of all the different gadgets. The children will enjoy playing with them, finding out what they are used for and trying to work out how to use them. Once the children have had a chance to experiment and talk amongst themselves, gather the class together and encourage the children to name the different objects and explain what they do. Introduce words like chop, grind, slice, grate, mince, press, squeeze. The children can then make up a kitchen song, incorporating the new words they have learnt.

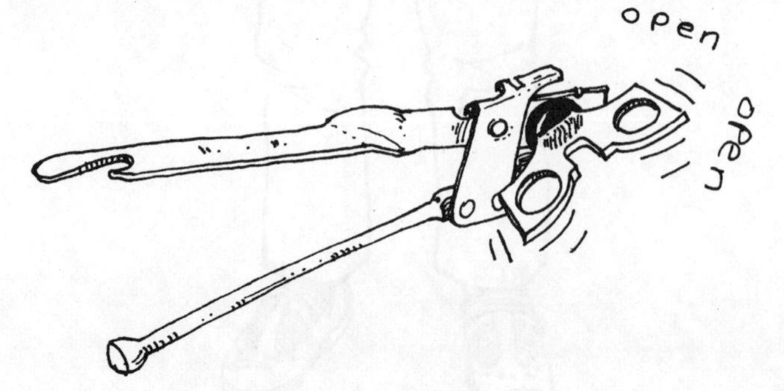

Here's the tin opener.
What can it do?
It opens up the tins for you.

Here's the pestle.
What can it do?
It pounds up lots of spices for you.

Here's the colander.
What can it do?
It drains off all the water for you.

Here's the peeler.
What can it do?
It skims off vegetable skins for you.

Here's a sharp knife.
What can it do?
It slices up the food for you.

Follow-up
Try concentrating on the sounds the gadgets make. Ask a small group of children to close their eyes while you (or another child) uses one of the gadgets. The children have to try to guess which gadget it is from the sound it makes. Encourage the children to describe and imitate the different noises. (J A Lindon's poem 'Sink Song' is a lovely starter.)

Alternatively, the children can use the tune of 'Here We Go Round the Mulberry Bush' and put kitchen words to it, eg 'This is the way we whisk our eggs/grate our cheese/mince the meat/slice the beans/cut the bread/peel the potatoes/squeeze out juice on a cold and frosty morning!'

What have I got?

Age range
Five to nine.

Group size
Whole class.

What you need
Ask the children to bring in something from home (obviously it shouldn't be valuable and needs to be fairly small).

What to do
The children bring in a special object which they keep secret and hidden from the rest of the class who will have to guess what it is. Each child can think up a clue to give to the other children, such as: it's made of wood, it's square and you can build with it (a wooden building block or brick); it's metal, you can push it along, it's a toy and it rhymes with star (car); it's got handles, you turn it and then jump over it (a skipping rope).

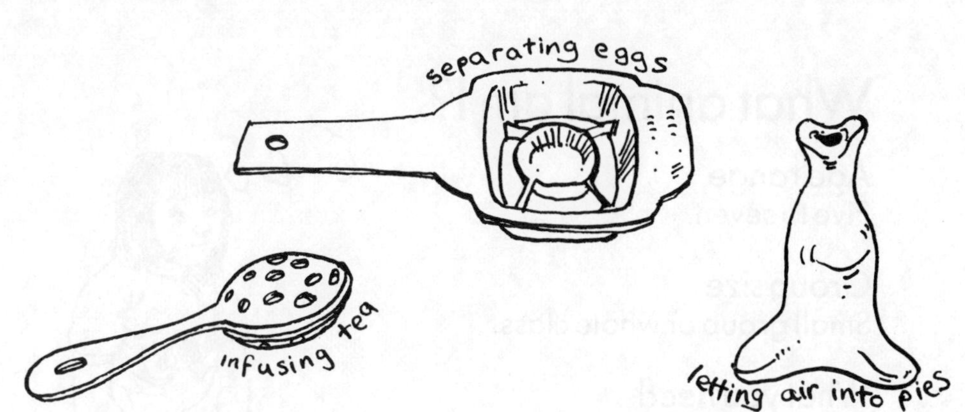

What can we use this for?

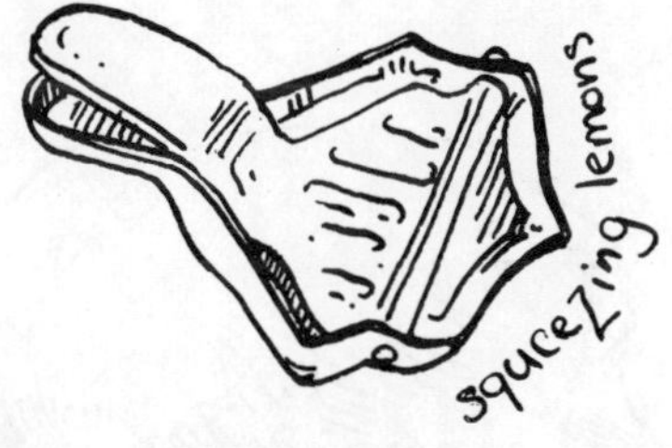

Age range
Five to nine.

Group size
Small group, ie five or six children.

What you need
A bag, box or sack filled with lots of different objects, eg a screwdriver, a nail file, a tin opener, an egg whisk, a torch.

What to do
The children sit in a circle with the mystery bag in the middle. They take it in turns to reach in and pull something out, and then talk about it, rather than just name it. The children may need a little help to get going – questions like 'What is it made of?' and 'What could we use it for?' will all help, and details like colour, shape, weight, texture can all be introduced.

Follow-up
The children might like to bring in their own 'mystery' objects from home (eg tea infusers, butter pats). Identify them and then think up new ways of using them.

What animal am I?

Age range
Five to seven.

Group size
Small group or whole class.

What you need
Model zoo or farm animals, or pictures of animals.

What to do
Start with a general discussion about different types of animals and how we can describe the differences between them. Depending on the age and experience of the children, you can introduce some slightly technical vocabulary, such as webbed feet, cloven hoofs, mammal, quadruped, etc. Once the children are familiar with the various terms, they take turns to choose an animal and then describe it to the rest of the class without showing it or giving its name. The rest of the children have to guess what it is from the clues, eg it has four legs, it eats grass, it has a mane. Whoever gets the right answer first then goes on to choose the next animal.

Tell me about this animal

Age range
Five to seven.

Group size
Small group or whole class.

What you need
Models or pictures of zoo and farm animals.

What to do
This game is really a variation of the one on page 26. Again, start with a general discussion about the various animals and reinforce any new technical vocabulary. You (or a helper) then stand at one end of the classroom or playground with the children lined up at the other end. Hold up a picture or model of an animal and ask, 'What can you tell me about this animal?'. The children take it in turns to say something, eg 'It is a cow', 'It gives us milk', 'It eats grass', 'Its baby is called a calf'. Each child who offers a new correct statement takes one step forward, and the first child to reach the teacher is the winner.

What's the same and what's different? 1

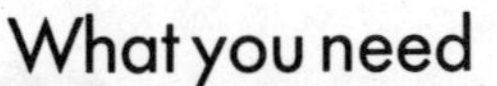

Age range
Seven to nine.

Group size
Small or large group.

What you need
The pictures used in the 'Where do I belong?' game (see page 9).

What to do
Hold up two pictures from any of the main groups, eg a pair of gloves and a pair of sandals. Ask the children, 'What's the same about these things?', hoping for the answer, 'They're things we can wear; they're clothes. We put them on'. Then ask, 'What's one thing that is different about them?' The answer might be, 'We put gloves on our hands and shoes on our feet', or, with prompting, 'We put gloves on when it's cold but we wear sandals in the summer'. Someone may offer colour, shape, etc, as examples of differences.

Follow-up
Divide the children into category groups (ie food, clothes, toys, etc) and ask them to sort their pictures according to different criteria. For example, the food group could use sweet/sour, fresh/cooked as the basis on which to sort the cards; the clothes group could use cold/warm weather, indoor/outdoor clothes, clothes with/without fasteners.

What's the same and what's different? 2

Age range
Five to nine.

Group size
Small group, ie five or six children.

What you need
Pairs of objects (or pictures of objects) that can be compared with one another.

What to do
Sit in a circle with the children and hold up two objects (or pictures of objects) that can be compared, eg an apple and a ball. Ask: 'What's the same about these two things?' – 'They're both small'; 'What's the other thing that's the same about them?' – 'They're both round'; 'What's the difference between these two things?' – 'One's an apple and one's a ball'; 'What's one other thing that's different between them?' – 'One's red and the other's blue'; etc.

The game can be made more difficult by comparing increasingly similar things, eg two farm animals, so that the children have to make finer and finer distinctions, and also learn to classify by function, size, colour, shape, texture, etc.

One more thing

Age range
Five to nine.

Group size
Small group, ie five to eight children.

What you need
Pictures of animals or other objects, and a cardboard post-box.

What to do
The children sit in a circle with the box in the middle. One of the children goes to the box, takes out one of the pictures and then goes back to his/her place in the circle, but stays standing up. He/she shows the picture to the rest of the group and then has to describe it, eg 'It's a bike, it's got two wheels, it's shiny'. Each time he/she gives a description, he/she takes a step forward until he/she reaches the box and drops the card in. The next child then finds a card and the game begins again.

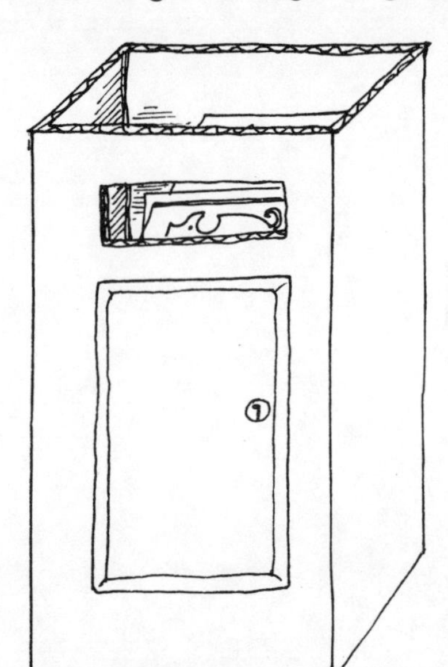

I'm thinking of . . .

Age range
Five to nine.

Group size
Small group, ie five or six children.

What you need
Posters of scenes.

What to do
One of the posters is spread out or pinned up in front of the group. One child chooses an object in the picture but doesn't tell the others what it is. The rest of the group then have to try to guess the object from the clues which the first child gives, eg 'I'm thinking of something in this picture . . .'.

The child then goes on to give clues of colour, size, shape, function, position, etc, until the other children guess what the object is.

What kind of people?

Age range
Five to seven.

Group size
Small group, ie five to eight children.

What you need
Photos/illustrations of people, or a Happy Families card game.

What to do
The cards or drawings are placed face down in a pile in the middle. One of the children picks up a card and identifies it, eg 'the boy'. The next child has to add another word – eg 'the little boy', and the next another word – 'the sad little boy' – and so on until everyone has had a turn. Then another child picks up the next card in the pack and the game continues.

Opposites

Age range
Five to seven.

Group size
Whole class.

What you need
No materials needed.

What to do
Probably the easiest way for children to grasp the idea of opposites is through plenty of examples. Once the children have grasped the concept, encourage them to supply some of the well-known examples, eg big/small, fast/slow, noisy/quiet, old/new, stop/go, full/empty, live/dead.

Once the children are quite confident and have had plenty of examples, ask them to see if they can find five opposites in the classroom – eg old/new books, noisy/quiet children, open/shut drawers – or in the playground, or on their way to school – eg old/new buildings, big/small dogs, fast/slow cars, quiet/noisy streets, full/empty buses, live/dead plants.

Family pairs

Age range
Five to seven.

Group size
Small group, ie five or six children.

What you need
Magazines or colour supplements, or pencils/crayons and paper.

What to do
A way of extending the idea of opposites is to play Family Pairs. The children can cut out from magazines or draw different sorts of people, both pairs and opposites, eg boy/girl, mother/father, grandfather/grandmother, brother/sister, young/old, happy/sad, strong/weak, short/tall, fat/thin, asleep/awake.

Follow-up
This activity could link up with the games on page 18. The children could compare their self-portraits and labels and list or link the pairs.

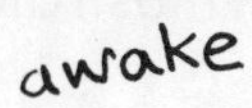

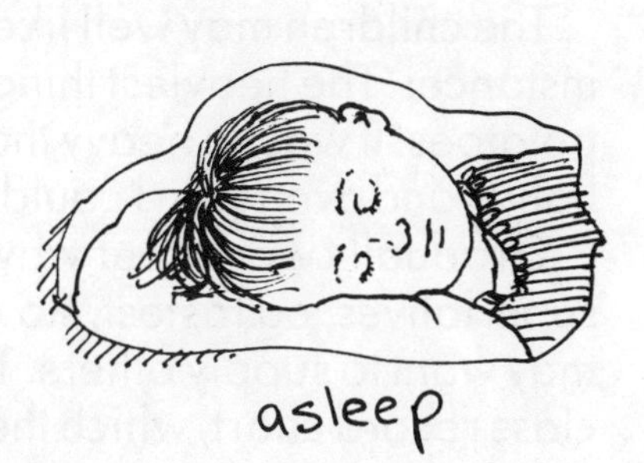

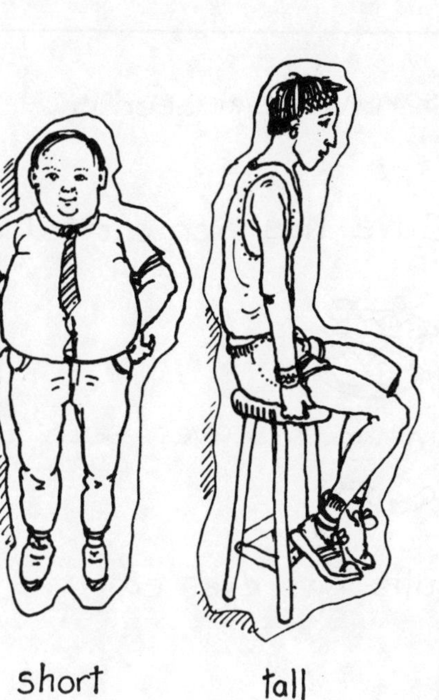

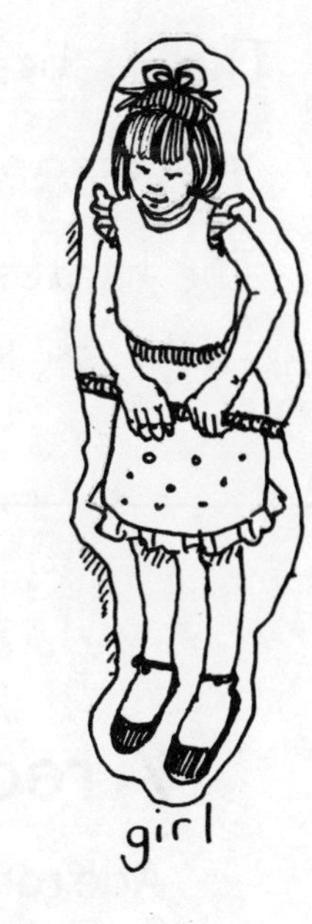

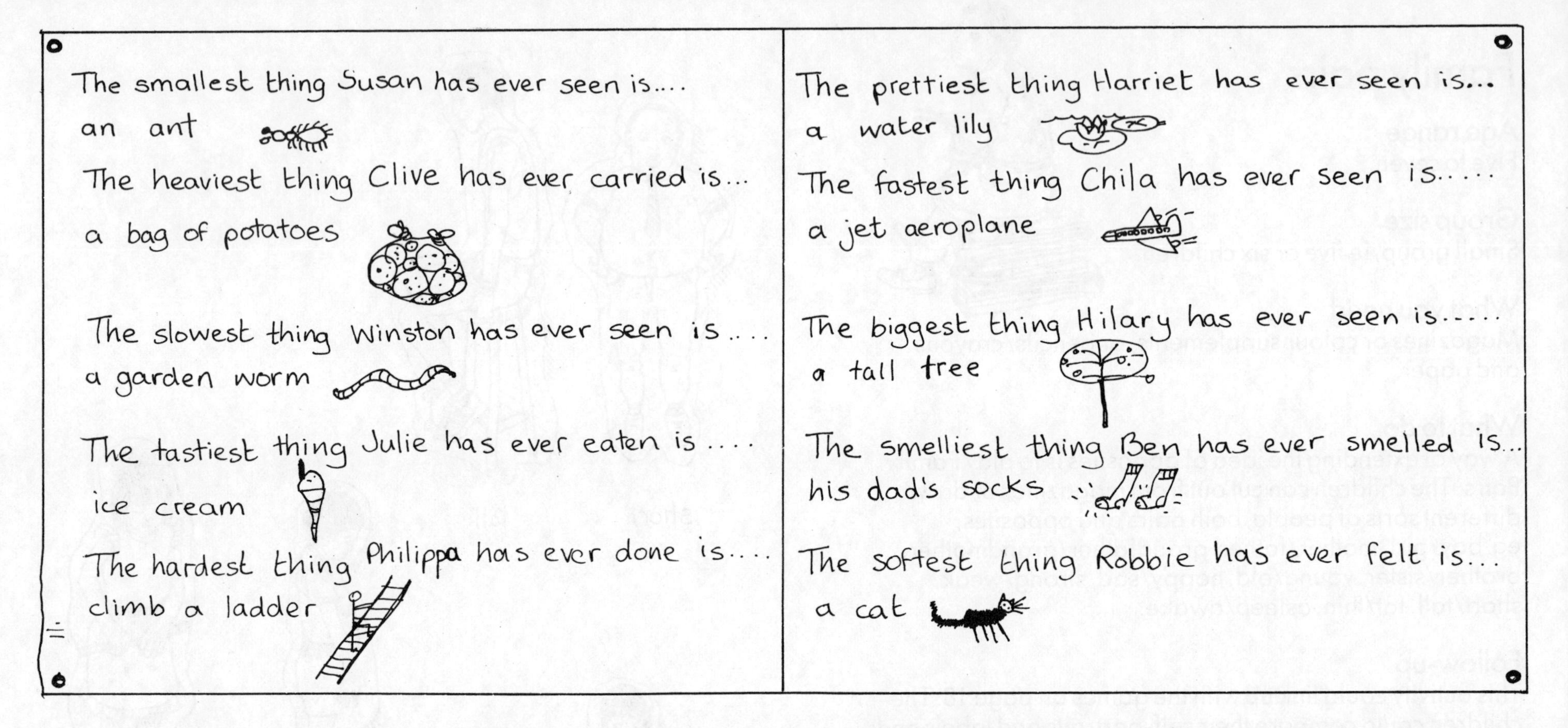

A record chart

Age range
Seven to nine.

Group size
Small group, ie five or six children.

What you need
A large piece of paper and a felt-tipped marker.

What to do
Ask the children to finish sentences like: 'The smallest thing I've ever seen was . . .'; 'The heaviest thing I've ever carried was . . .'; 'The prettiest thing I've ever seen was . . .'.

The children may well like to expand on their ideas, for instance: 'The heaviest thing I've ever carried was a bag of potatoes. It was so heavy that I had to pick it up with two hands and even then I couldn't really carry it'.

Gradually work your way through the most common superlatives, eg fastest, slowest, biggest – the children may want to supply others. Together you can then make a class record chart, which the children can illustrate.

Happy families

Age range
Seven to nine.

Group size
Whole class.

What you need
No materials essential but Rod Campbell's *Great, Greater, Greatest* is a useful starter.

What to do
Following on from 'A record chart' on page 34, introduce the idea of comparatives and superlatives, ie big, bigger, biggest; small, smaller, smallest; happy, happier, happiest.

Once the children have grasped the concept, ask them to get into groups of three and invent a family, eg the Happy or Sad family. Each group can then take it in turn to mime their name and the rest of the class have to guess what it is. For example, with the Happy family, one child would be Miss or Master Happy, one would be Mrs Happier and the remaining child would be Mr Happiest.

Follow-up
A variation on this game is to give each child a part, eg Master Sad, Mrs Taller. They then have to go round the class, find the rest of their family and stand in order, ie sad, sadder, saddest; tall, taller, tallest.

Add a bit more

Age range
Seven to nine.

Group size
Small group, ie five to eight children.

What you need
No materials needed.

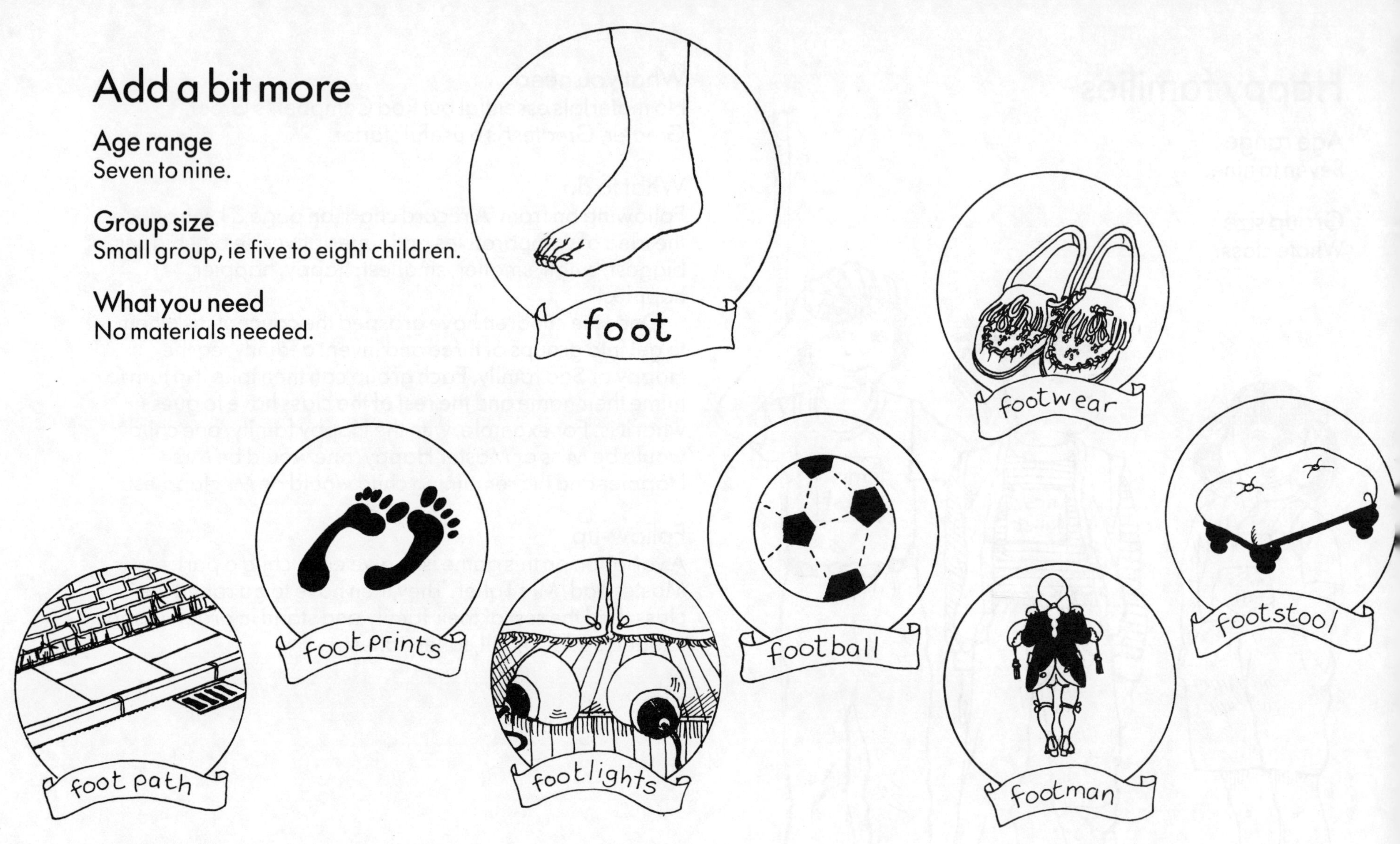

What to do
Sit with the children in a circle. Choose a word and ask the children in turn to add a bit more to make a new word, eg shoe: shoelace, shoeshop, shoebox; door: doorstep, doorstop; bed: bedroom, bedside, bedbug; motor: motor car, motorway; foot: football, footstep; fire: fireplace, fireman, fireball, firebird, firearm, fireguard.

Follow-up
Once the children are happy about making new nouns, encourage them to make other parts of speech, eg kind: kindness, kindly; sick: sickness, sickly. This will prepare them for the games involving suffixes – see page 38.

Find your partner 1

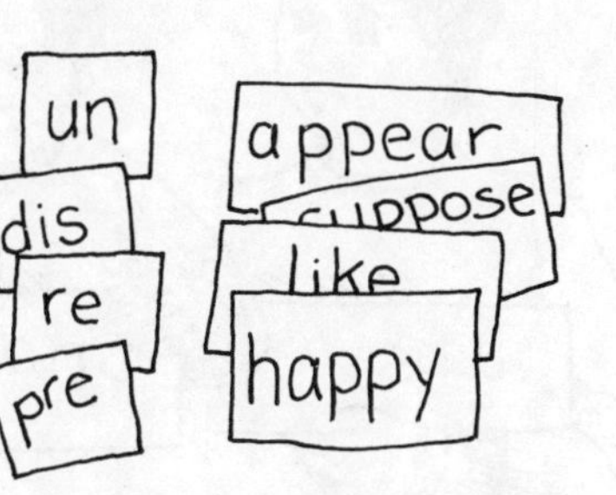

Age range
Seven to nine.

Group size
Large group or whole class.

What you need
A number of cards with prefixes written on them – the exact number will depend on how many children are playing the game. The easiest ones to start with are un-, dis- and re-. The rest of the group are given cards with words which can be added to the prefixes to make new words, eg happy (unhappy), kind (unkind), appear (disappear/reappear), like (dislike), do (redo, undo).

What to do
Give each child a card. The children with the prefix cards go and stand in different parts of the room. The other children look at their cards (make sure they can all read them) and then have to find the right prefix and stand by their partner. When all the children have found a partner, take each group in turn and ask the children to say the new word they have made. Discuss possible alternatives, eg reappear/disappear, undo/redo.

Follow-up
The children could make charts to go on the wall, showing the words they have made and adding new ones as they come across them.

Older or more able children could work with the more difficult prefixes, eg im-, sub-, en-.

Find your partner 2

Age range
Seven to nine.

Group size
Large group or whole class.

What you need
A number of cards with suffixes written on them (start wi -less, -ful and -ness) and other cards with words which c be added to the suffix cards to make new words, eg kin (kindness), happy (happiness), hope (hopeless), care (careless), wonder (wonderful).

What to do
The procedure is exactly the same as for 'Find your partner 1'. Once all the children have found a partner, go through the new words they have made and see if the children can work out what some of the suffixes mean, eg 'less' means without or a lack of something; 'ly' makes an adjective into an adverb.

Follow-up
Keep the children in their groups and ask them to compile a list of all the words they can think of ending in their particular suffix. The group with the most words is the winner.

Find your partner 3

Age range
Seven to nine.

Group size
Large group or whole class.

What you need
Cards showing root words, prefixes and suffixes, eg un kind ness, dis courage ment, re place ment, un favour able.

What to do
Give each child a card. The children with root cards stand in separate corners of the classroom. To make the game a little easier to start with, pair up children with appropriate prefixes and suffixes (eg un/ness, dis/ment, dis/able) who then go off to find a suitable root word.

Follow-up
Once the children are familiar with the game, make it slightly more difficult by not pairing up the prefixes and suffixes, reducing the number of root words and playing a version of Musical Pairs. Whoever hasn't found an appropriate partner by the time the music stops is out.

Word rummy

Age range
Seven to nine.

Group size
Small group, ie three to five children.

What you need
A pack of root, suffix and prefix cards as used in 'Find your partner' (page 38).

What to do
Deal each of the players five cards. The rest of the cards are placed face down in a pile in the middle. The players have to try to make words from the cards they hold in their hands. They can use root cards with a prefix, or suffix, or both. Each player takes it in turn to discard a card and pick one up from the central pile. When a player has a word he/she places it face up and replaces the cards from the central pile. The player who makes the most words is the winner. A player can add to a word he/she has put down, eg he/she can add 'ment' to 'replace'. Any player who puts down an incorrect word forfeits a go.

Follow-up
The game can be made easier by just using prefixes and root words or suffixes and root words, or more difficult by having to use all three.

A variation is to use the same cards to play Pelmanism as on page 11.

Winter words

Age range
Seven to nine.

Group size
Whole class.

What you need
No materials essential, but an appropriate poster or illustration of wintry weather or a wintry scene would help create the right atmosphere.

What to do
Invite the children, one at a time, to 'Try to make us feel cold'. They may come up with phrases like 'icy frosty fingers creeping', 'wintry winds whistling and wailing' or 'cold snow slipping down the back of your neck'. Once the class has been sufficiently chilled, other children could be asked to 'Warm us up again, please' with 'hot, steaming bowls of soup' or 'flickering flames and friendly fires'.

Encourage the children to use different inflections to underline the meaning of the words. If they haven't already noticed the part played by alliteration, point it out to them. They might then like to make up a 'cold' story, either working in small groups or with each child adding a sentence.

Follow-up
This game can be adapted to suit different seasons and situations, eg 'Make us feel hot/sad/scared'. The children might like to paint, mime or dance some of the most effective replies.

Food, glorious food

Age range
Five to nine.

Group size
Whole class.

What you need
No materials essential, but some useful starters are 'The Centipede's Song' from chapter 18 of Roald Dahl's *James and the Giant Peach*, or 'Mad Meals' and 'Mad Drinks' from Michael Rosen's *Quick, Let's Get Out of Here*.

What to do
Ask the children to make up menus for different feasts or special occasions – the more sumptuous and bizarre the better. Some ideas to help them get going are: the Iron Man's breakfast, Fungus the Bogeyman's birthday party and The Ugly Bug Ball. A witches' Hallowe'en party could have a menu of fried frogs' legs, nauseous navarin of newt, spider soufflé, roast rat with putrid potatoes, etc. The Great Emperor of China's wedding feast could consist of roast bird of paradise with bamboo shoots and marigold buds, grilled goldfish in firefly sauce, etc.

Follow-up
The children might like to write out menus of the most popular ideas and decorate them. Older children could make up recipes for some of the more bizarre items, eg cereal for the Iron Man's breakfast. Ingredients: 20 rolls of barbed wire, 10 litres sump oil. Soak barbed wire overnight in oil. In the morning, break wire into bite-sized pieces, garnish with nuts and bolts and serve immediately.

STORY STARTERS

Stories without words

Age range
Seven to nine.

Group size
Small group, ie five or six children.

What you need
A collection of picture-books without words, eg Raymond Briggs' *The Snowman*, Shirley Hughes' *Up and Up*, Jan Ormerod's *Moonlight* and *Sunshine*, and any of John Goodall's picture-books, for example *An Edwardian Christmas, Jacko, The Surprise Picnic.*

What to do
Picture-books without words can be an excellent stimulus for story-telling. The material can be used in several ways: two children can take turns in telling the story into a tape-recorder, each perhaps doing a page at a time; a group of children can take it in turns to describe a picture each, with you or another adult writing down what they say; several children could work together to invent a story based on the first few pictures and then make up their own ending.

Follow-up
A particularly exciting version of the story could be recorded on tape or written down so that other children can 'read' it along with the pictures.

Story starters

Age range
Five to nine.

Group size
Any size.

What you need
No materials needed.

I hate it when I have to go to bed when the sun is shining.

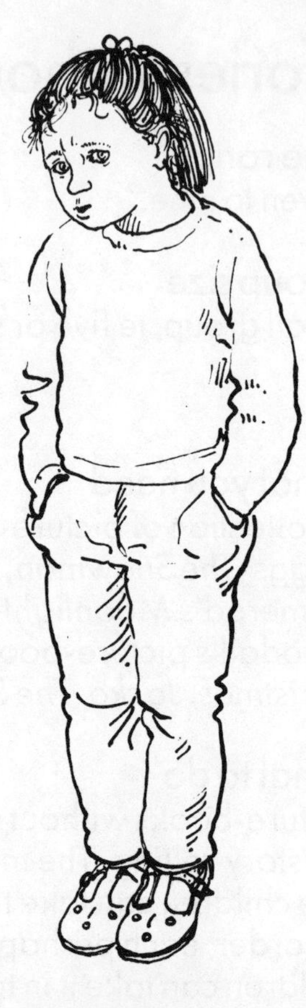

What to do
There are several different ways to give children a starter for imaginary stories. Try using illustrations, reading from an exciting story and stopping at a particularly gripping moment, displaying other children's art work, asking children to think up endings for current television serials, or offering an opener like: 'I hate it when I have to . . .'; 'What makes me really angry is when . . .'; 'One day my dog did something really strange, he . . .'.

The children may prefer to tape their stories, or particularly successful ones could be written down later. They may prefer to work in groups or individually, with each child contributing just a few sentences.

Telling a story

Age range
Seven to nine.

Group size
Individual children, pairs of children, or whole class.

What you need
A cassette tape-recorder.

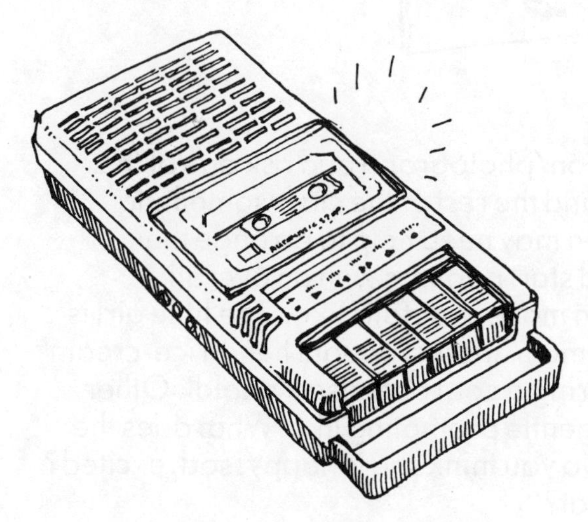

What to do
You (or a parent helper/fluent child reader) read a story on to one side of a cassette. The other side is left blank for children to record their version of the story, retold in their own words.

Another variation is for you to start reading a story to the class but break off at an exciting point. A child, or group of children, then takes the book, reads the ending and retells it in his/her own words on cassette which can then be played back to the rest of the class.

A cassette can also be used to replace the traditional news session on Monday morning. During the day, the children can take it in turns to talk about what they have done at the weekend. At the end of the day the resulting tape can be played back to the whole class. Individual children can be asked to expand on any items which catch the other children's interest.

What do you see?

Age range
Five to nine.

Group size
Whole class.

What you need
Several illustrations or photographs.

What to do
Hold up an illustration/photograph and ask one of the children to tell you and the rest of the class something about it. The children may need help to arrange their thoughts: they could start perhaps with an overall description and then move to details like, 'The little girl is happy because her mum has just bought her an ice-cream' or 'Everyone is wearing a coat because it's cold'. Other children may need gentle prompting like 'What does the little girl feel like? Do you think she is happy, sad, excited? Why do you think that?'

Follow-up
A variation on this activity is to show two fairly similar pictures at once, eg two pictures of children playing. One of the children chooses one of the pictures to describe and the rest of the class have to guess which one it is from the description alone.

Before and after stories

Age range
Five to nine.

Group size
Small group, ie five or six children.

What you need
Posters/pictures/illustrations of a lively scene or event which could act as a basis for story-telling.

What to do
The children look carefully at the pictures and talk about what is happening – they may give names to the characters, decide what time of the day/year it is, which country it is, etc. One half of the group then makes up the 'before' story to explain what happened leading up to the picture, and the other half of the group makes up the 'after' story to carry on from where the picture finishes.

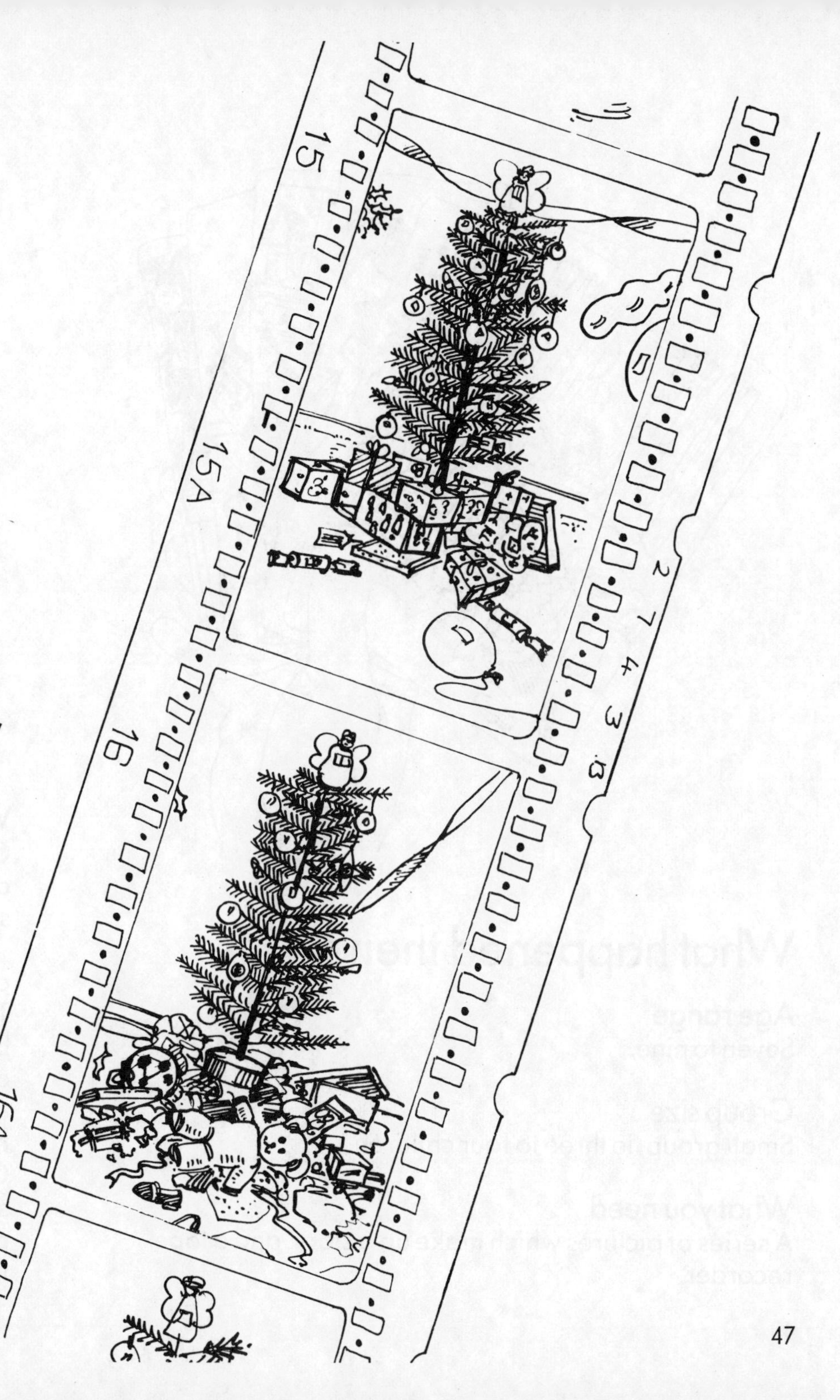

What happened then?

Age range
Seven to nine.

Group size
Small group, ie three to four children.

What you need
A series of pictures which make up a story, and a tape-recorder.

What to do
Give two of the children the set of cards. They have to decide on what they think is the right order and make up a story, based on the cards, which they then record.

The cards are then shuffled and given to the other children who decide on what they think is the right order. They check their version against the original by playing back the tape, or if they prefer they can make up a different story.

Follow-up
Once the children have mastered the idea of putting stories into logical sequence, they can work in groups or pairs putting short stories which have been broken down into paragraphs back into the correct order.

Group stories

Age range
Seven to nine.

Group size
Small group, ie six to eight children.

What you need
No materials needed.

What to do
The children sit together in a circle. In the middle there is a box containing cards with adjectives written on one side (eg scary, funny, sad, long, short) and an illustration of the adjective on the other side (eg a laughing face for funny, a crying face for sad). One child reaches into the box and pulls out a card. If it is the funny card, the group have to make up a funny story, with each child in turn adding a sentence until the story is completed. If the story begins to falter, or when it is complete, the next child reaches into the box and pulls out another card and the story-line then has to be changed to fit the new adjective.

Sound stories

Age range
Seven to nine.

Group size
Whole class or small group.

What you need
No materials needed.

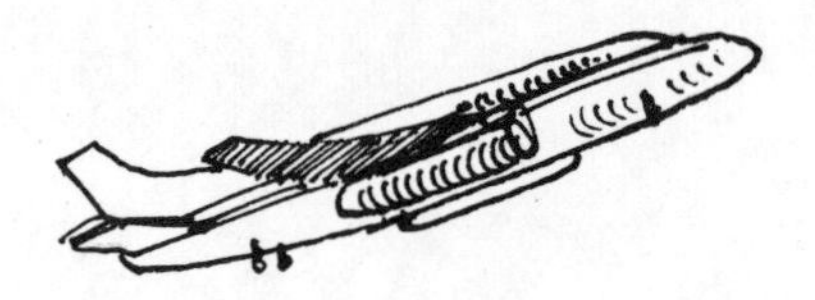

What to do
Either you or a parent/helper can take a small group of children on a 'sound walk'. Explain to the children beforehand that the idea is to concentrate on what they hear rather than what they see. Encourage them to close their eyes from time to time (obviously not in the middle of a road or a busy pavement!). When you get back to the classroom, talk about what you heard and build up a store of sound words. The children can then make up a story based either on sounds they heard or on imaginary sounds. These stories could be put on tape, accompanied by appropriate sound effects.

Alternatively, the children could concentrate on sounds in the classroom, again by closing their eyes and listening carefully. These sounds could then be used as the basis of a story.

Follow-up
Younger children often enjoy listening to tapes of familiar sounds (eg kettle whistling, police car siren, telephone ringing) which they could then try to identify.

The treasure box

Age range
Five to nine.

Group size
Small group, ie five or six children.

What you need
A treasure box made from a cardboard box covered with felt or silk and studded with jewels of silver foil, painted shells, beads, etc, with a hole cut in the side, and treasure such as a sponge soaked in scent, wrapped in foil and then in velvet.

What to do
The children take it in turns to be blindfolded or close their eyes and then put a hand into the treasure box. They feel (and in the case of the example given, smell) the treasure which they then describe: 'It's squeezy', 'It smells like flowers', 'It's scrunchy and crinkly', etc. Different treasures will encourage descriptions based on different senses; for smell, try pot-pourri or oranges studded with cloves.

Follow-up
A favourite variation on this theme is the Nelson's Eye game. Peeled grapes (eyes), a wet sponge (brain), a carrot (finger), a balloon filled with cold water (heart), etc, are passed round a circle of blindfolded children as macabre accessories to a ghostly story made up by one of the children who acts as narrator.

Mysterious stories

Age range
Five to nine.

Group size
Small group, ie five or six children.

What you need
A large bag containing interesting objects that could be used to start off a story, eg a key, a pebble, a feather and a map.

What to do
The children sit in a circle with the bag in the middle. They take it in turns to pull an object out of the bag and make up a story about it.

A variation on this theme is for one child to pull something out, begin a story about it and stop at a given signal. Then the next child has to take over the story, pull out another object and weave it into the plot. The game can finish either when each child has had a go, or when there are no more objects left in the bag, or when the story has come to an end.

'Spook when you're spooken to . . .'

Age range
Five to nine.

Group size
Whole class.

What you need
A suitably ghastly spook – either a picture painted by the children, or made from a piece of old sheet with hideous felt features.

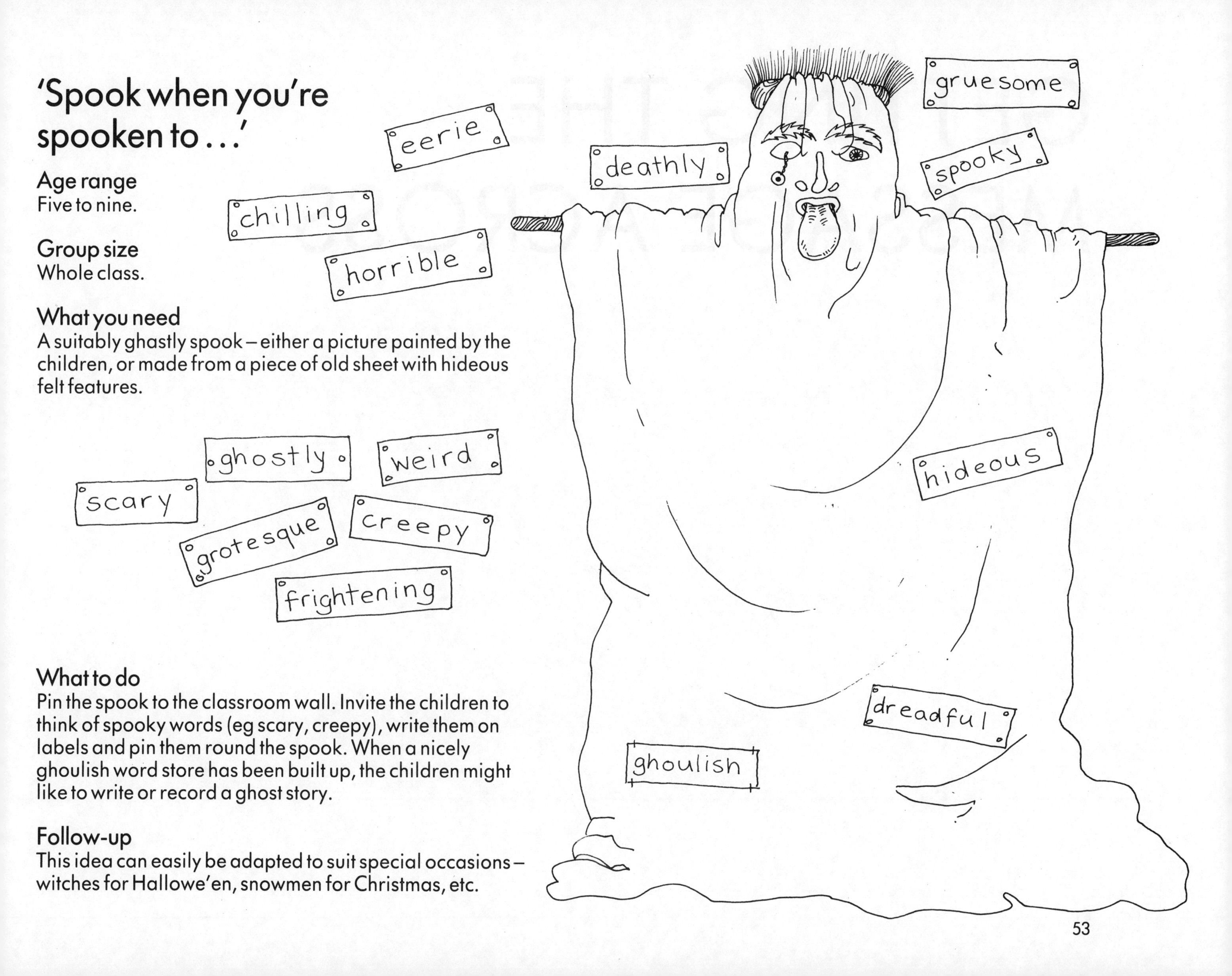

What to do
Pin the spook to the classroom wall. Invite the children to think of spooky words (eg scary, creepy), write them on labels and pin them round the spook. When a nicely ghoulish word store has been built up, the children might like to write or record a ghost story.

Follow-up
This idea can easily be adapted to suit special occasions – witches for Hallowe'en, snowmen for Christmas, etc.

GETTING THE MESSAGE ACROSS

Miss Muddle

Age range
Five to nine.

Group size
Whole class.

What you need
Pictures – either specially drawn or cut out from magazines.

What to do
Explain to the children that today you are Miss (or Mr) Muddle and that you keep getting everything muddled up – especially what you say. Ask the children to help you unmuddle your mistakes. You can then show them a picture of, for example, a girl riding a bike and say something like 'The bike is riding a girl'. The children usually enjoy putting you right and once they have got the idea of the game, the jumbled sentences can become slightly more complex, eg 'Girl riding is the bike'.

the bike is riding the girl

Mr Topsy-Turvy

Age range
Five to nine.

Group size
Small group, ie five or six children.

What you need
No materials essential. It may help to prepare a story in advance if you aren't keen on improvisation, or if there are certain parts of speech on which you want the children to concentrate.

What to do
Explain to the children that you are going to tell them a story about Mr Topsy-Turvy, who keeps getting things muddled up. They must listen carefully and help you correct all the mistakes.

Early one morning Mr Topsy-Turvy set out for work. The moon (sun) was shining brightly as Mr Topsy-Turvy got under (into) his car, turned the engine off (on) and drove down the river (road). He stopped at the penguin (pelican or zebra) crossing to let Mrs Happy and Elizabeth, her son (daughter) cross, etc . . .

Follow-up
This type of story can be used to focus on particular parts of speech such as prepositions, verb tenses, adverbs, etc.

The mixed-up game

Age range
Five to nine.

Group size
Small group, ie five or six children.

What you need
No materials needed.

What to do
Explain to the children that today you are Miss/Mr Muddle who keeps getting everything all mixed up. Ask the children if they can help you get things right. So, for example, if you say, 'James is crying', James has to say, 'No, I am not crying'; if you say, 'Samia is not wearing a blue dress', Samia has to reply, 'Yes, I am wearing a blue dress'.

Again, once the children have got the hang of the game, you can make it progressively more difficult by building up, for example, to, 'The goldfish are in the gerbil's cage'.

Follow-up
Sing or chant the following rhyme with the children:

Lazy Mary, will you get up, will you get up, will you get up,
Lazy Mary, will you get up, will you get up today.
No Mother, I won't get up, I won't get up, I won't get up,
No Mother, I won't get up, I won't get up today.

You can then adapt it to suit your class, eg:

Noisy James, will you be quiet . . . today.
No teacher, I won't be quiet . . . today.

Lazy Zahid, will you clear up . . . today.
No teacher, I won't clear up . . . today.

The children sing the reply. You can, of course, alter the response to:

Yes teacher, I will clear up . . . today!

This makes sense 1

Age range
Five to nine.

Group size
Whole class.

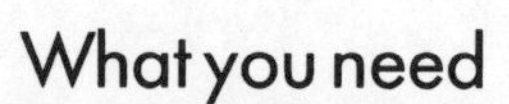

What you need
Pictures of nouns (people and animals are easiest) and verbs (eg a picture of someone skipping, crying or laughing).

What to do
The children have to invent sentences based on the pictures you hold up. For example, if you hold up a picture of a girl and another picture of someone crying, the children might say 'The girl is crying' or 'The girl cried' or 'The girls cried' – the verb tense is not as important as the combination of subject and verb.

The game can be made slightly more difficult by asking the children to supply an adverb, eg 'The girl cried loudly' or 'The girl cried bitterly', and an adjective, eg 'The sad girl cried loudly'.

Follow-up
The game can be made more interesting if the children make a television out of a large box by cutting out a screen and making slots to feed through the strips of paper with the nouns and verbs on them.

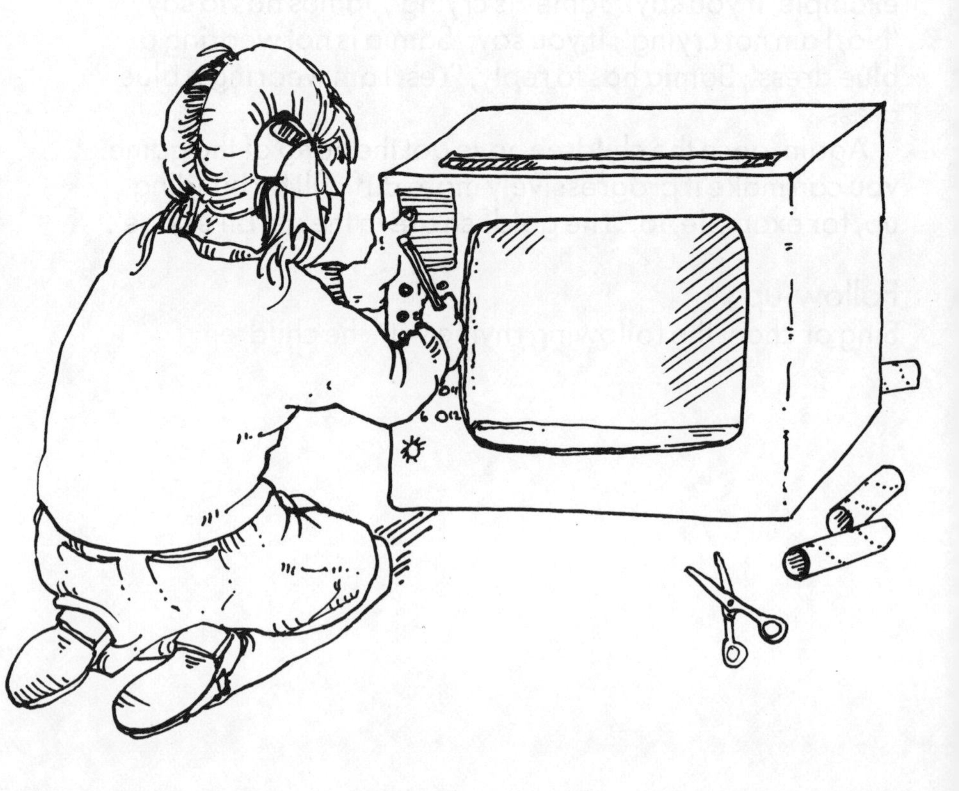

This makes sense 2

Age range
Seven to nine.

Group size
Small or large group.

What you need
Pictures of nouns (people and animals) and verbs on strips to be fed through the television described on page 58.

What to do
As in 'This makes sense 1', the children have to make up a sentence based on the strips being fed through the television. The variation here is to introduce a mismatch between the adjective and adverb. For example, you feed through a picture of a girl smiling to give the subject and adjective – 'the happy girl' or 'the friendly girl' – followed by a picture of a girl crying to give the verb and adverb – 'cries bitterly' or 'sobs loudly'. The children have to point out the incongruity between adjective and adverb and choose a picture which does make sense by matching the subject/adjective picture.

The Grumpies

Age range
Five to seven.

Group size
Small group, ie five or six children.

What you need
No materials needed.

What to do
You and the children sit in a circle. Explain that today they are going to be the Grumpies – cross, grumpy people who spoil everything you say. So, when you say 'It is a lovely day today', the Grumpies reply, 'It is not a lovely day today'. If you said 'It is fun to play this game', the Grumpies' reply would be, 'It is not fun to play this game', etc. Once the children have got the hang of the game, you can gradually make it more difficult, eg 'Is it a warm day today?' – 'It is not a warm day today'; 'Are you enjoying this game?' – 'We are not enjoying this game'.

Follow-up
Try playing the yes/no game. You (or the children) ask a willing victim questions. He or she must answer without using the words yes or no: eg 'Do you like eating ice-cream?' – 'I do like eating ice-cream'; 'Is your name Rehan?' – 'My name is not Rehan' or 'That is not correct'.

What is it?

Age range
Five to nine.

Group size
Small group, ie five to eight children.

What you need
A box containing about eight familiar objects, eg a shoe or a brick.

What to do
Show the objects to the children and ask them to say what they are called, using the 'What is this?' 'It's a shoe' construction.

Once the children know the names of all the objects, one child comes out, chooses something from the box and keeps it hidden from the rest of the group. The other children then have to try to guess what the object is by asking 'Is it a shoe or a sock?' etc, until they get the right answer. Meanwhile the child with the object has to use the 'No, it isn't a shoe or a sock' construction. When someone does get the right answer, he replies, 'Yes, it's a shoe', or whatever.

Where are you ?1

Age range
Five to seven.

Group size
Small group, ie five to eight children.

What you need
A large picture/poster of a busy park or playground scene, either a commercially-produced one or one prepared as follow-up material for the 'Teacher's taking me to the park tomorrow' activity (see page 70).

What to do
Show the children the poster. If it is a commercially-produced one, ask them each to choose one of the people illustrated and give them a name. You then give a series of clues (all based on prepositions) and the children have to track down the person or object, eg

Who is swinging up in the air?
Who is standing on top of the wall?
Who is hiding under the bush?
Who is sitting next to the tree?
What is in front of the bench?
Who is behind the slide?

Follow-up
Nursery rhymes like 'The Grand Old Duke of York', 'Incy Wincy Spider', 'Little Miss Muffet', etc, can be sung by the youngest children. An indoor follow-up for older children is the 'Hunt the slipper' activity on page 63.

Where are you ?2

Age range
Five to seven.

Group size
Whole class.

What you need
A skipping rope.

What to do
Take the children into the playground and play games that will reinforce the prepositions they have learnt indoors.

A good skipping game is Under the Moon and Over the Stars. Two children turn the rope. The rest of the class line up and take it in turns to go 'under the moon' (ie they run under the rope) or 'over the stars' (ie they jump over the rope), depending upon the instructions given by the turners.

Another skipping rhyme which also teaches months of the year is Birthdays. Again, two children turn the rope and call out 'Come in when it's your birthday'. They then chant the months of the year and the children run in and start skipping when their month is called. When all the children are in (or when it gets too crowded!) the turners shout 'Go out when it's your birthday', give the months again, but this time the children run out.

Stand the children in a circle by asking, 'Shazia, you stand next to James. Wesley, you stand next to Shazia', etc. Ask certain children to stand inside or outside the circle. Then sing 'In and out the windows' as the children walk round the circle weaving in and out. Stop them at intervals and ask, 'Sharon, who is behind you?'; 'Christos, who is in front of you?'; 'Layla, who is opposite you?', etc.

Hunt the slipper

Age range
Five to nine.

Group size
Any size.

What you need
No materials needed.

What to do
Decide in advance on prepositions that the children need to practise, eg in, under, on, behind, beside, above, below.

One of the children hides an object (eg a book) in, under or on something while the rest of the class close their eyes. They then have to ask him/her where it is, eg 'Is the book under the table?', 'Is the book in the cupboard?', 'Is the book on the floor?'. Whoever gets the right answer then hides the book in, under or on something else, or behind/beside it, etc.

Follow-up
You can make up a Mr Topsy-Turvy story which concentrates on prepositions (see page 56). Vinyl stick-on figures and scenes can provide useful practice for individual children. To begin with, it helps if you (or an adult helper) sit with the child and ask him/her to put the little girl in the kitchen/beside the stove/on top of the bed, etc. Once the children are more confident you could put such requests on tape.

Why?/because 1

Age range
Five to nine.

Group size
Small group, ie five to nine children.

What you need
No materials.

What to do
Introduce the why/because construction by singing or chanting the following nonsense rhyme:

Why can't a dog climb an apple tree,
Why, oh why, oh why?
Because, because, because, because,
Goodbye, goodbye, goodbye.

You can adapt the first line to suit you and the children, eg 'Why can't a pig drive a motor car?', 'Why can't a cat play a violin?', 'Why can't a snake do a jigsaw?'. Alternatively, older children may prefer any of the many 'Why did the chicken cross the road' jokes. The important thing is to give constant repetition of the why/because cause and effect sequence.

Once the children have mastered the construction, ask the questions individually, eg 'Why are you wearing a jumper, Nima?' – 'Because it is cold today'. 'Why are you smiling, Nurinder?' – 'Because I am happy'. You can then move on to more open-ended cause/effect questions: 'Why is the boy in the picture running?' – 'Because he is late for school/being chased by a lion/wants to catch the bus'. 'Why do we clean our teeth?' – 'Because we need to get all the food off', etc.

Follow-up
Ring the changes by offering children the cause, eg 'Because her tooth hurts', and asking them to supply the effect, 'Why is the little girl crying?' or 'Why is the little girl unhappy?', etc.

Why?/because 2

Age range
Five to seven.

Group size
Small group, ie five to eight children.

What you need
A television as described on page 58, and cause and effect strips, with drawings on, to feed through the slots.

What to do
Sit the children where they can see the screen. Feed in cause and effect strips, eg a picture of a girl falling over (cause) and a picture of a girl crying (effect). Invite one of the children to tell what is happening, eg 'The girl is crying because she has fallen over/hurt herself'; 'The boy is laughing because the clown is doing funny tricks'; 'The children are indoors because it is raining'; 'The car has stopped because the traffic lights are red'.

Follow-up
Give pairs of children shuffled sets of cause/effect cards and ask them to match up the right causes and effects.

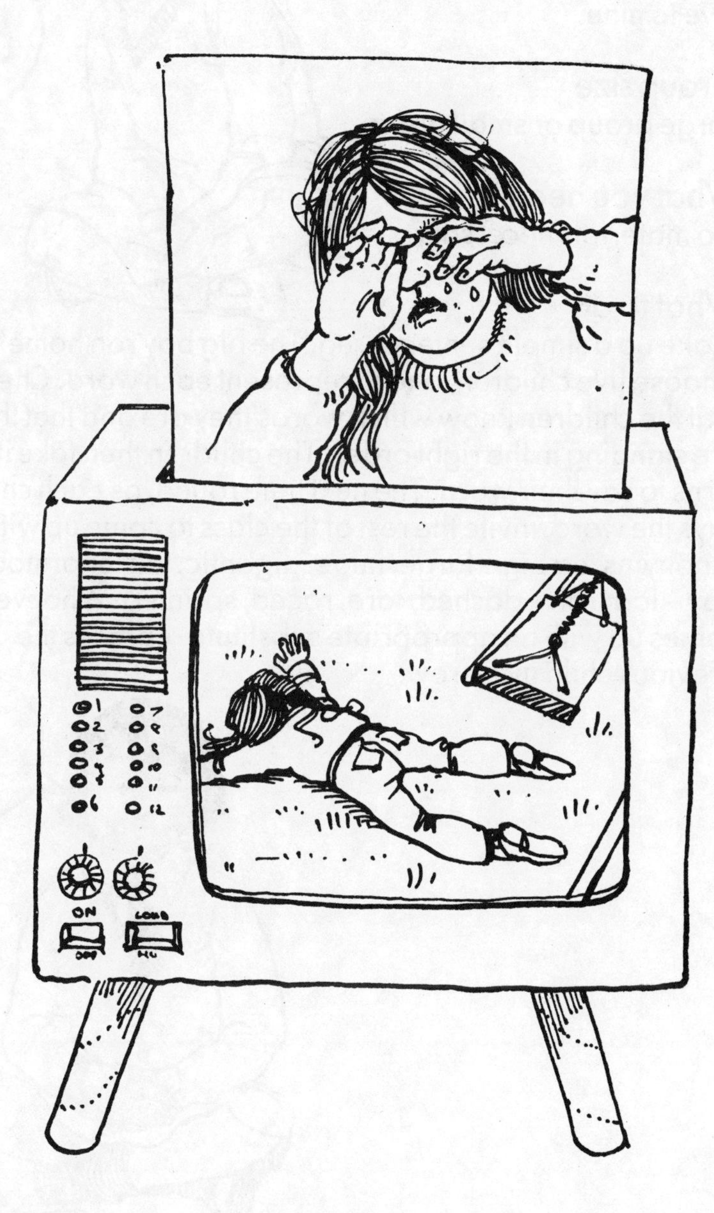

All change places

Age range
Five to nine.

Group size
Large group or small group.

What you need
No materials necessary.

What to do
Make up a simple sentence, eg 'The big boy ran home'. Choose five children, one to represent each word. Check that the children know which words they are and that they are standing in the right order. The children then take it in turns to say their word. The next time round, as each child says the word, invite the rest of the class to come up with synonyms, eg big – large, huge, gigantic, tall, enormous; boy – lad; ran – dashed, tore, raced, sprinted. Whoever comes up with an appropriate substitute replaces the previous child in the row.

Follow-up
An easy version of the game is to muddle up the words so that they are standing in the wrong order, eg home boy big ran the. The rest of the class then has to put them back into the right sequence. To make the game more difficult you can either make the sentences longer or ask the children to supply opposites rather than synonyms, eg 'The big boy ran home' might become 'The small girl dawdled to school'.

Who did what where how?

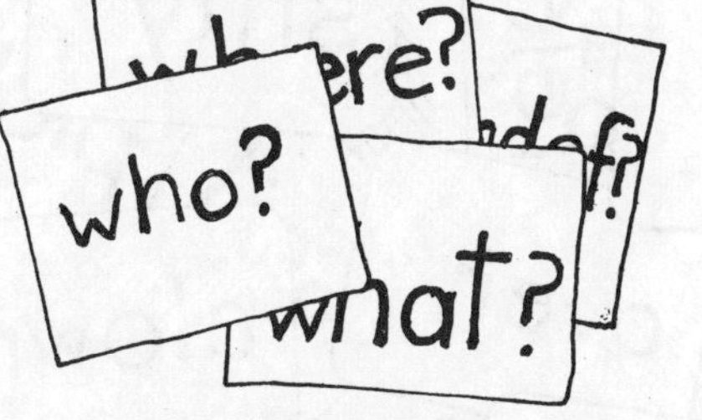

Age range
Seven to nine.

Group size
Large group or whole class.

What you need
Cards, each of which shows one of the following questions: Who? Did what? How? Where? When? Why? What kind of?

What to do
This game is a variation of 'All change places', on page 66. Again, choose children to come out and stand in a row representing parts of a sentence. This time, instead of each child representing a word, some will be given question cards instead. The rest of the class take turns to provide answers to the questions and replace the question-card children in the row. In this way, sentences can be expanded by adding new parts of speech while keeping the basic correct word order.

To begin with, introduce one question card at a time, eg the girl saw a 'what?' (ghost); the girl saw a 'what kind of?' ghost (hideous); the girl saw a hideous ghost 'where?' (by her bed); the girl saw a hideous ghost by her bed 'when?' (at midnight); the 'what kind of?' girl saw a hideous ghost by her bed at midnight (scared); the scared girl saw a hideous ghost by her bed at midnight 'why?' (because her room was haunted).

Follow-up
With older children (or with younger ones who have had plenty of practice) you can introduce as many question cards as you like straight away, but give the children a particular theme to work on, eg funny, scary or wintry. Alternatively, you can give them an opening sentence and ask the children to use the row to keep the story going bit by bit.

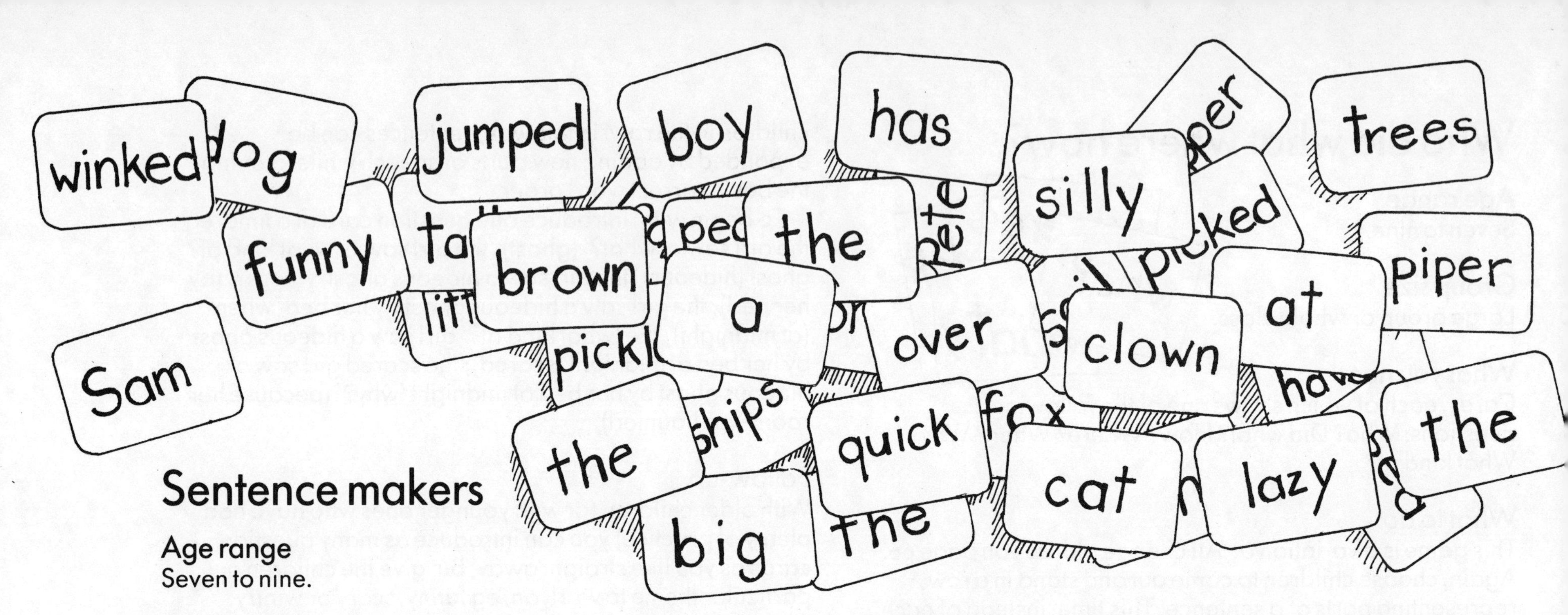

Sentence makers

Age range
Seven to nine.

Group size
Small group, ie three or four children.

What you need
Simple sentences written on card and cut up into individual words, eg little Sam has a big cat; the funny clown winked at the silly boy; the quick brown fox jumped over the lazy dog. (Avoid using capital letters.)

What to do
Shuffle the word cards, then give the group one sentence at a time. Ask the children to make as many sentences as they can using all the words, eg little Sam has a big cat; big Sam has a little cat; has big Sam a little cat?; has little Sam a big cat?

When the children have finished rearranging the words, ask them to write down, or put on tape, all their variations. These can be used by other groups to see if there are any permutations they have missed.

Slogans – the good and the bad

Age range
Seven to nine.

Group size
Whole class, divided into groups of approximately five or six.

What you need
No materials needed.

What to do
Each group is given a word (eg eggs) and has to write a slogan for it, using the letters to make an acrostic. Each group can decide whether they want to write a pro- or anti-slogan. For example a pro-egg slogan might be: Eggs Give Great Strength; an anti-egg slogan might be: Eggs – Ghastly Glutinous Substances.

Follow-up
Obviously it is wiser to start with short words. Food is a good topic. Once the children have got into the swing of it, try longer words and other categories like animals (pro- and anti-cat and dog slogans), pop groups, makes of car, or football teams.

The best slogans could be made into full-scale advertisement posters.

Teacher's taking me to the park tomorrow

Age range
Five to nine.

Group size
A maximum of eight children per adult (willing parents could be invaluable).

What you need
Any local park with a playground.

What to do
Before the visit, make sure the children have the basic vocabulary to describe the various activities, eg swinging, climbing, sliding. Once at the park, concentrate on practising the various tenses by asking questions and receiving answers: 'What are you doing?' – 'I am swinging'; 'What are you going to do now?' – 'I am going to climb'; 'What have you been doing?' – 'I have been running'.

Follow-up
Make a park picture. The children can paint pictures of themselves, stick them on the appropriate part of the scene and label them, eg 'Nima is swinging', 'Rehan is climbing', 'Samia is running'. The labels could be changed each day to reinforce the different tenses, eg 'Nima was swinging' or 'Nima swung on the swing'; 'Rehan was climbing' or 'Rehan climbed'; 'Samia was running' or 'Samia ran'; 'Nima is going to go on the swings'; 'Rehan is going to climb'; 'Samia is going to run' or 'Samia will run'.

Beep beep

Age range
Five to eleven.

Group size
Whole class.

What you need
No materials needed.

What to do
Someone is chosen to be 'it' and leaves the room while the rest of the class decides on what is going to be 'beep beep'. This can be any activity like swimming, singing, riding, laughing, walking, eating or washing. When 'it' returns to the classroom, he/she tries to guess what 'beep beep' is, by asking yes/no questions, eg 'Can you beep beep outdoors?' 'Do you beep beep at night?' 'Can you beep beep anywhere?' 'Can an animal beep beep?'

When 'it' guesses what 'beep beep' is, he/she swaps places with the child who answered the last question. If 'it' cannot guess the answer, he/she can ask the class for three clues, eg 'You beep beep when you see a funny film'; 'You beep beep when you're happy'.

Can you do it beepily?

Age range
Seven to nine.

Group size
Whole class.

What you need
No materials needed.

What to do
This is a variation of the 'Beep beep' game on page 70, but instead of choosing an activity, whoever is 'it' decides on an adverb, eg happily, grumpily, quickly, slowly. The rest of the class then has to guess what the adverb is by asking 'it' to do something 'beepily', eg 'Will you sing beepily', 'Will you walk beepily'. The first person to guess what 'beepily' is then becomes 'it'.

Follow-up
Younger children whose vocabulary is more limited might enjoy acting out this rhyme and trying to find adverbs to describe the different ways they have to move:

When I was a lady, a lady, a lady,
When I was a lady, this is how I went . . .

When I was a farmer . . .

When I was a princess . . .

When I was an old man . . .

When I was a toddler . . .

When I was feeling happy . . .

When I was feeling tired . . .

What's wrong with me?

Age range
Five to nine.

Group size
Whole class or large group.

What you need
No materials needed.

What to do
Doctors and Nurses is an all-time favourite game with most children. This variation uses their morbid fascination with illness to introduce and reinforce certain basic vocabulary and constructions.

You (or one of the children) mime some sort of ache, eg tummy ache, headache, toothache, and then ask 'What's wrong with me?' hoping to draw out the reply 'You've got tummy ache' (or whatever is appropriate). Once this particular construction has been mastered, the children can move on to variations such as 'You've got a sore throat' (rather than 'You've got throat ache') or 'You've got something in your eye' (rather than 'You've got eye ache'). The question can be changed to 'What's the matter with my eye?' to introduce constructions like 'It hurts', 'It's hurting' or 'It's sore'.

Follow-up
Once the children have mastered the basic constructions, they might like to launch into a fully-fledged game of doctors, complete with dramatic telephone calls from anxious parents!

Younger children can learn 'Miss Polly Had a Dolly' and take it in turns to play the part of Miss Polly and the doctor.

1 Miss Polly had a dolly who was sick, sick, sick,
2 So she sent for the doctor to come quick, quick, quick.
3 The doctor came with his bag and his hat,
4 And he knocked at the door with a rat-a-tat-tat.
5 He looked at the dolly and he shook his head.
6 He said, 'Miss Polly , put her straight to bed!'
7 He wrote out a prescription for a pill, pill, pill,
8 'I'll be back in the morning, yes I will, will, will'.

These are the actions to go with the song:
1 Children rock the dolly in their arms.
2 Children mime telephoning the doctor.
3 Children mime being the doctor.
4 Children mime knocking on the door.
5 The doctor looks at the doll – shakes his head.
6 The doctor shakes his finger at Miss Polly.
7 The doctor writes a prescription.
8 The doctor waves goodbye.

I went to the chemist and I bought . . .

Age range
Five to nine.

Group size
Whole class or large group.

What you need
Bandages, sticking plasters, pills, medicines, drops, disinfectant – all, of course, carefully supervised and then safely put away.

What to do
Begin with a class discussion and demonstration of various first-aid techniques, eg bandaging, putting on plasters, cleaning cuts, taking medicines, pills. Then the children can play 'I went to the chemist and I bought . . .', with each child taking turns to mime an item which the rest of the group have to guess. As each item is identified, the children can add it to their list, chanting 'I went to the chemist and I bought a bandage, some sticking plasters, a bottle of medicine . . . '.

Follow-up
The children could make a giant chemist's window and fill it with bottles of medicine or pills, with their names and suggested doses written on them.

What would you do if? 1

Age range
Seven to eleven.

Group size
Whole class, organized into small groups of three to six children.

What you need
No materials needed.

What to do
Explain to the class that you are going to give them a problem. The idea is not to find just one obvious solution but to try to come up with as many different ideas as possible within a time limit of ten minutes. One member of each group will be responsible for jotting down the ideas. Try the following problems:

A man has a house on the corner of the street. It has a beautiful garden but no fence round it. Every morning a huge dog takes a short cut across the garden instead of walking round on the path. What can the man do?

Take the class outside into the playground. Allow them five minutes' play and then bring them back into class. Give the groups ten minutes to come up with ideas on how to make the playground more fun.

Show the children a glass jar or bottle. Ask them to imagine they have 12 such jars. What could they do with them?

Follow-up
These sample problems can be followed by any of your own choosing (the children may come up with their own suggestions). A group could go round the school with a tape-recorder and interview other children to get their responses and make charts or graphs of the most common/unusual replies.

What would you do if? 2

Age range
Five to nine.

Group size
Whole class.

What you need
No materials needed.

What to do
Give the children an imaginary problem and ask them to come up with ideas on how to solve it.

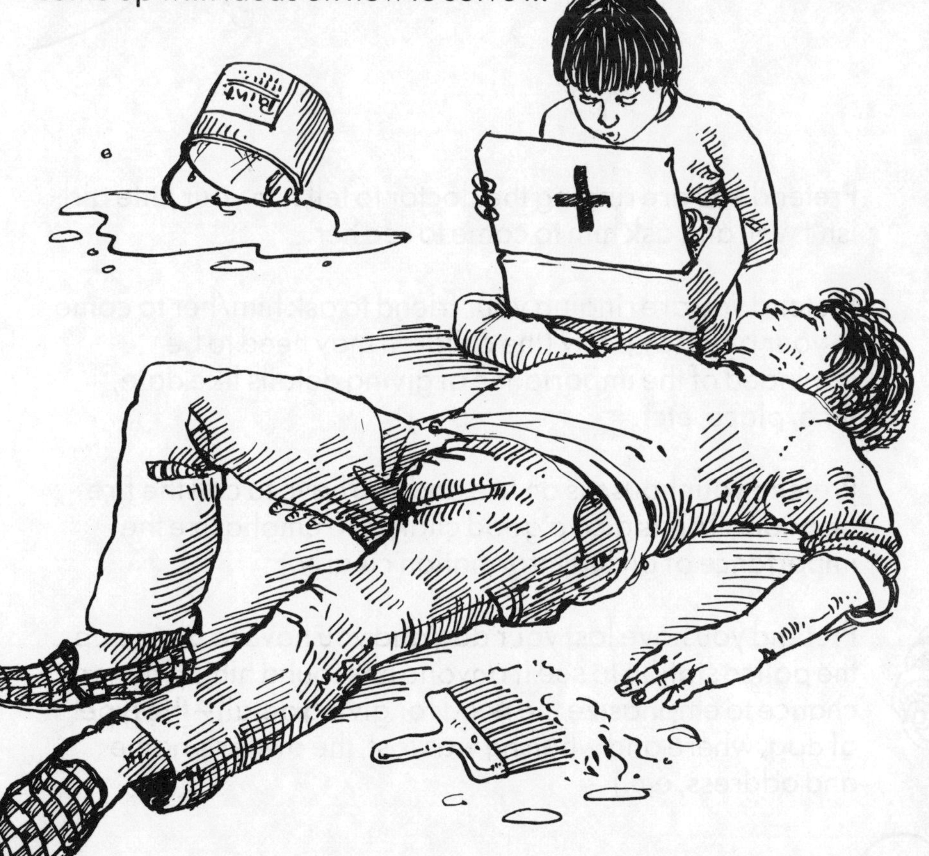

What would you do if you lost your Mum in a crowded shop?

What would you do if your Dad had an accident at home and you were the only person in the house?

What would you do if you got stuck in the lift in a block of flats?

What would you do if your Mum forgot to come and collect you from school?

Encourage the children to discuss the various solutions put forward. Would they work?

Follow-up
John Burningham's *Would You Rather . . .* is another good starter to encourage children to give reasons for their choice of action. In this case it might be best to have the children work in pairs or small groups, and record on tape their different choices and reasons for them. The whole class could then listen to the tape and discuss the different replies.

Telephone talk 1

Age range
Five to nine.

Group size
Small group or pairs of children.

What you need
Toy telephones.

What to do
The idea is to simulate real conversations and to teach the children how to use the telephone in an emergency. To begin with, it helps if the children have some concrete suggestions to get them started:

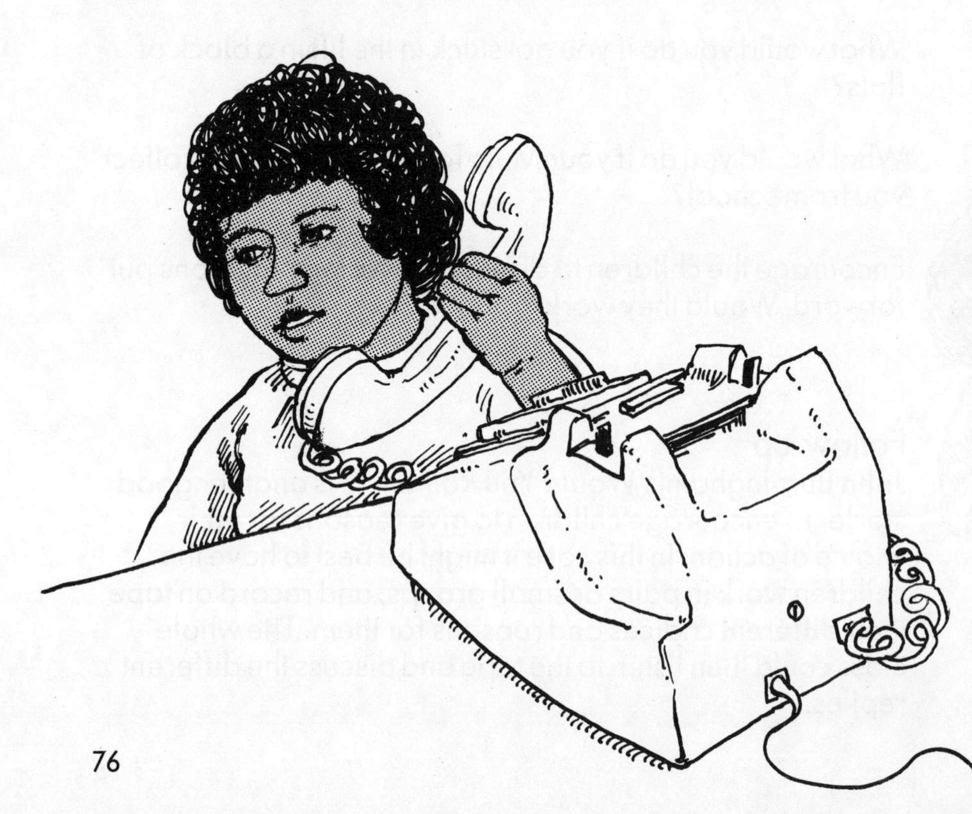

Pretend you are ringing the doctor to tell him your little girl isn't well and ask him to come to see her.

Pretend you are ringing your friend to ask him/her to come to your birthday party (the children may need to be reminded of the importance of giving details like date, time, place, etc).

Pretend your house is on fire and you have to call the fire brigade. (This is also a good chance to emphasize the importance of giving information clearly.)

Pretend you have lost your dog and you have to phone up the police station to see if anyone has found him. (This is a chance to emphasize the need for giving detail – the type of dog, where and when he was lost, the owner's name and address, etc.)

Telephone talk 2

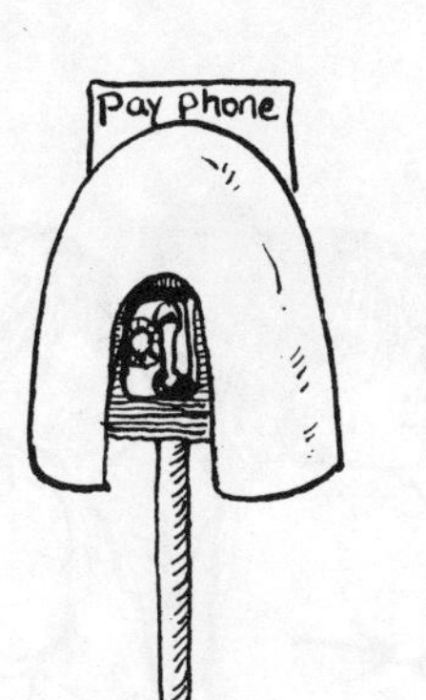

Age range
Seven to nine.

Group size
Pairs, or a maximum of four children.

What you need
Access to a telephone.

What to do
Ask the children to find out a specific piece of information which will involve using the telephone. Here are some examples of what they might find out:

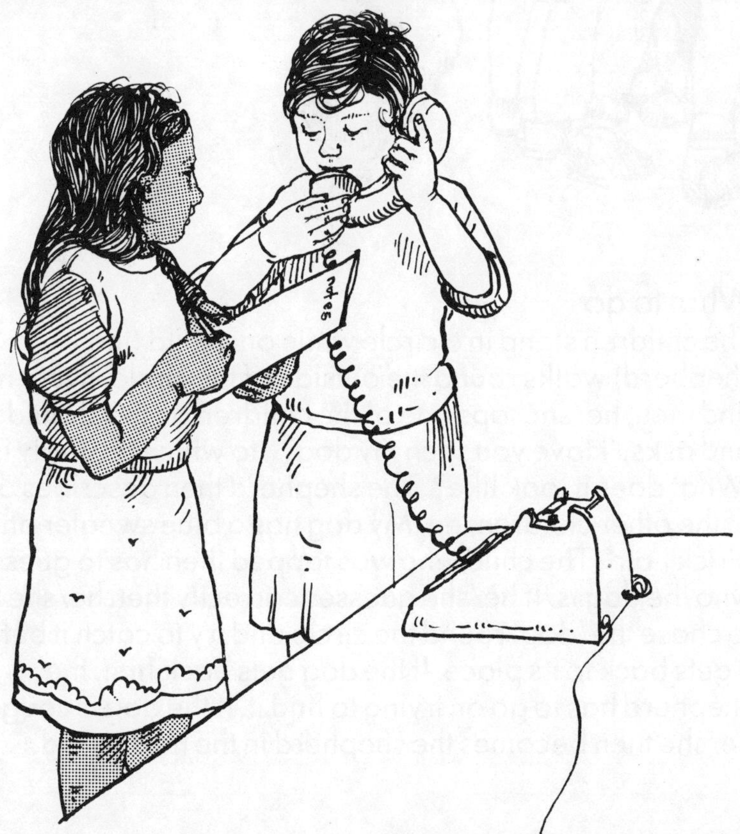

The opening times of the local swimming pool, with details of reduced-price sessions for children.

The performance and running time of a children's matinee at a local cinema, together with prices for children's tickets.

The opening and closing time of a particular exhibition at a museum, together with admission prices.

The train timetable for a school journey.

An unlisted telephone number from Directory Enquiries.

The children may need help with looking up and dialling certain numbers, but they should be encouraged to work out what they need to ask and how to do this on their own.

Follow-up
Once the children have successfully reported back with the information, they might like to make a tape for younger (or less confident) children describing what they did, in what order, and offering any useful pieces of advice, eg make sure you have a piece of paper to write down the information; it helps to write down the telephone number before you start dialling.

Sheep and shepherd

Age range
Five to nine.

Group size
Large group, ie ten or more players.

What you need
No materials needed.

What to do
The children stand in a circle while one child (the shepherd) walks round the outside of the circle. Every now and then, he/she taps one of the children on the shoulder and asks, 'Have you seen my dog?', to which the reply is, 'What does it look like?' The shepherd then describes one of the other children, eg 'My dog has a blue sweater and black hair'. The child who was tapped then has to guess who the dog is. If he/she guesses correctly then he/she has to chase the 'dog' round the circle and try to catch it before it gets back to its place. If the dog gets back first, the shepherd has to go on trying to find it. If the dog is caught, he/she then becomes the shepherd in the next round.

Mother/Father may I?

Age range
Five to nine.

Group size
Whole class.

What you need
No materials needed.

What to do
Whoever is chosen to be Mother/Father stands about ten metres away from the rest of the players. The object of the game is to be the first person to reach Mother/Father.

Mother/Father gives instructions to each child in turn about the number and kind of steps to take, eg giant steps, skipping steps, bunny hops, frog jumps, twirling steps, Superman steps, Incredible Hulk steps – and any others the children can think of. After Mother/Father says, for example, 'Sam, you can take four giant steps', Sam has to ask 'Mother/Father, may I?' The reply may be yes or no, but if Sam forgets to ask, he forfeits his turn and has to return to the starting line. The first child to reach Mother/Father takes over that role.

Simon says

Age range
Five to nine.

Group size
Whole class.

What you need
No materials needed.

What to do
This is a variation on the well-known party game. The children spread out so that they each have plenty of space and can see Simon (who could be you or a child). Simon faces everyone and gives orders: 'Simon says "Stand on one leg"', 'Simon says "Touch your nose"', etc. If the order does not begin with 'Simon says' any child who obeys it is out; the last child left is the winner and the next Simon.
To make the game more difficult, Simon can deliberately mismatch the order and the action, eg 'Simon says "Clap your hands"' while he puts his hands on his head. This will make sure that the children are listening rather than just copying the action.

Robots

Age range
Five to eleven.

Group size
Whole class.

What you need
A watch or egg-timer.

What to do
Choose two children; one will be the robot, the other the master. The master has to make the robot do a specific task (eg walk from the classroom door to the blackboard) inside a given time. The robot has to follow instructions to the letter and do only what the master tells him/her to do. The rest of the class have to watch to make sure that the robot obeys instructions. So the master has to give clear, accurate directions, eg 'Take two steps forward. Stop. Turn right and take five steps forward'. If the robot does something without being asked, or makes a mistake, both master and robot are out and another pair has a turn.

When the children first play the game, try being the robot yourself so that the children realize just how specific the instructions have to be.

This is what you do . . .

Age range
Seven to nine.

Group size
Whole class.

What you need
No materials needed.

What to do
Ask one of the children who has just mastered a new game (either one for the playground or an indoor board game) to tape or describe live how to play it. The other children then have to try to play the game using only the instructions which they have been given. The success or failure of the game will depend on the clarity of the instructions, and will bring home to the children just how detailed and accurate directions need to be.

Can you find me?

Age range
Seven to nine.

Group size
Pairs of children.

What you need
Pictures of food, clothes, animals, toys, etc, as in 'Where do I belong?' (page 9), and a tape - recorder.

What to do
Choose one of the older/more confident children and give him/her a random selection of cards from different categories. Ask him/her to tape a series of clues for another child to help him/her choose the right picture. Explain the importance of getting the sequence of information right. For example, it's important to start by saying what sort of thing the object is: 'This is something we eat. It's green. It's round. It's sweet. It's crunchy and juicy'. Only by listening to all the clues will the child work out that he/she needs the picture of an apple (all the previous clues could have referred to a grape as well). The children can work together to check the answers and talk about clues which weren't clear.

Find the treasure

Age range
Seven to nine.

Group size
Pairs of children.

What you need
A tape-recorder and treasure map. The map can either be drawn by you or the children, or be a collage made out of pictures cut from magazines. It needs to have plenty of detail – sharks, reefs, coves, porpoises, little pictures of wind characters with puffed-out cheeks, etc.

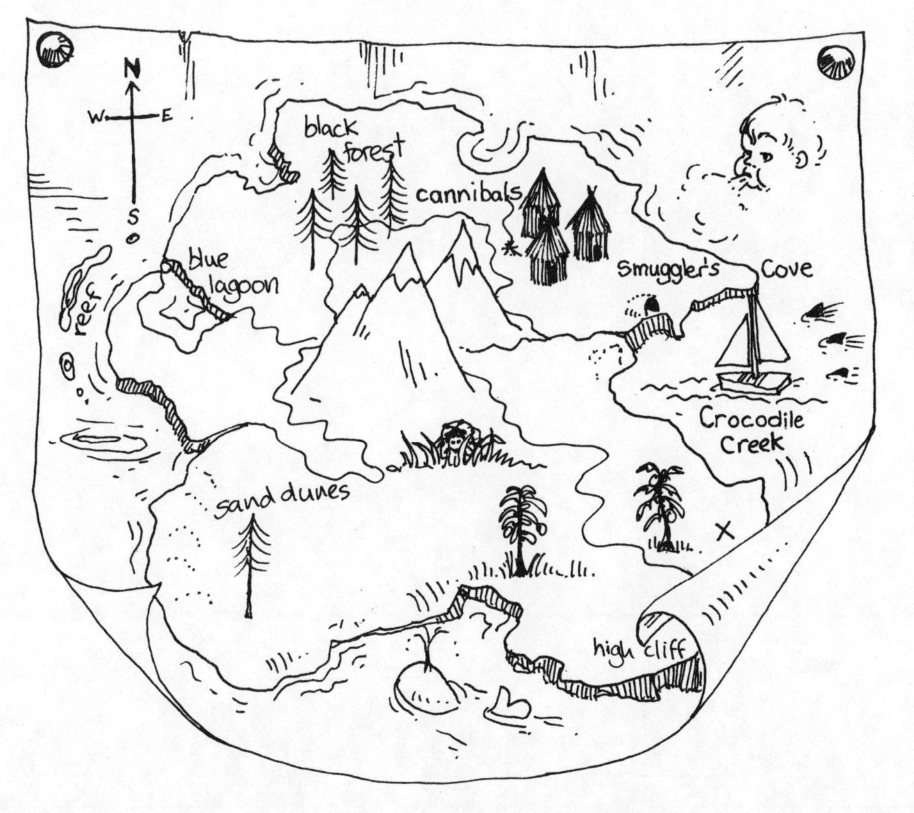

What to do
Give one of the children the map and ask him/her to decide where to bury the treasure. He/she then has to tape instructions telling the other child how to find it. Encourage detailed step-by-step instructions, eg 'Start at the bottom left-hand corner of the map. Sail to the West Wind. Turn right and sail to the first group of sharks. Turn left and head into the creek. Land at Smuggler's Cove and walk up along Crocodile Creek. Turn right at the second palm tree. Move 10 mm to your right and dig'. If the child plots his journey on a tracing-paper overlay, the children can check together that the instructions were followed, and if not, whether this was because they weren't clear.

Follow-up
An alternative version is to use a large-scale map of the local area. One of the children tapes detailed instructions on how to reach a particular place, but instead of giving its name says 'Where are you?' The other children take turns listening to the tape and write down where they ended up, eg 'I am outside the library'; 'I am outside the swimming pool'; 'I am by St Peter's Church'.

RHYMES, RIDDLES AND NONSENSE

Playground rhymes

Age range
Five to eleven.

Group size
Whole class.

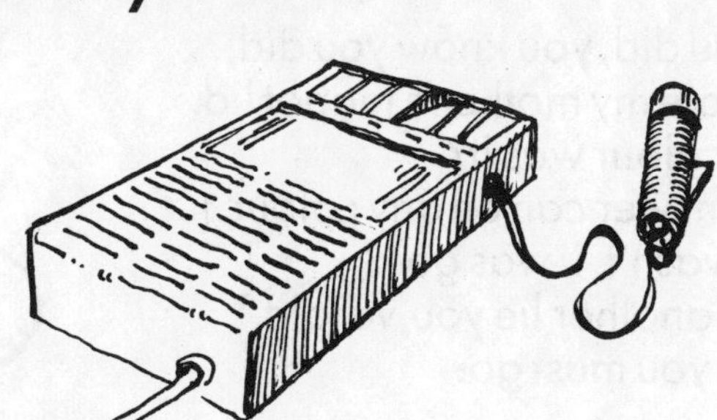

What you need
No materials essential, but a tape-recorder is handy.

What to do
Children usually have a fund of rhymes which are part of their games – dips, skipping rhymes, playground chants, rituals for making up after quarrels, etc. Ask the children to put their favourites on tape. Parents and other members of staff may be able to remember some they used as children; put those on the tape too. The resulting tape could be swapped with another school in a different part of the country to see what the regional variations are.

Follow-up
The children might be interested to hear some of the rhymes and chants from Michael Rosen's *Inky Pinky Ponky* or R A Smith's *Blue Bell Hill Games*. Iona and Peter Opie's book on *The Lore and Language of Schoolchildren* is the definitive adult source.

Dips

One potato, two potato, three potato, four,
Five potato, six potato, seven potato, more.

Ip dip sky blue,
Who's 'it', not you.
Not because you're dirty, not because you're clean,
My mother says you're the fairy queen
So out you must go.

Each peach pear plum,
Who's your best chum,
Not to be on 'it'.

Did you ever tell a lie?
No.
Yes you did, you know you did,
You stole my mother's teapot lid.
What colour was it?
(The answer can be any colour.)
No it wasn't, it was gold,
That's another lie you've told
So out you must go.

Dip, dip, dip,
My blue ship,
Sailing on the water,
Like a cup and saucer,
Out you must go.

Eenery meenery minery mo,
Tickle your tummy and tickle your toe,
If you laugh then out you go
And that means you.

Ipper dipper dation,
My operation,
How many people at the station?
The one who comes to number (whatever)
Will surely not be 'it'.

Skipping rhymes

Teddy bear, teddy bear, touch the ground,
Teddy bear, teddy bear, turn around,
Teddy bear, teddy bear, walk upstairs,
Teddy bear, teddy bear, say your prayers,
Teddy bear, teddy bear, turn out the light,
Teddy bear, teddy bear, say goodnight.

Nebuchadnezzar the King of the Jews
Bought his wife a pair of shoes,
When the shoes began to wear
Nebuchadnezzar began to swear,
When the swear began to stop
Nebuchadnezzar bought a shop,
When the shop began to sell
Nebuchadnezzar bought a bell,
When the bell began to ring
Nebuchadnezzar began to sing
Do re mi fa so la ti do.
(Whoever is skipping does the bumps until he/she is out.)

Drip drop down by the sea
Up popped a mermaid and she said to me,
Please Sir tell me the time,
Mind your own business it's half past nine (ten,
eleven, etc).
(Whoever is skipping does the bumps until he/she is out.)

As I was walking round the lake
I met a little rattlesnake,
I gave him so much jelly cake
I made his little belly ache,
One, two, three,
Out goes she (or he).

Eeny, meeny, miny, maw,
Erracle, terracle, tiny taw,
One, two, three,
Out goes she (or he).

Hickery dickery, six and seven,
Alabone, crackabone, ten and eleven,
Spin, span, muskidan,
Twiddle'um, twaddle'um twenty-one,
O U T spells out.

Rhyming words

Age range
Five to seven.

Group size
Whole class or group.

What you need
No materials needed.

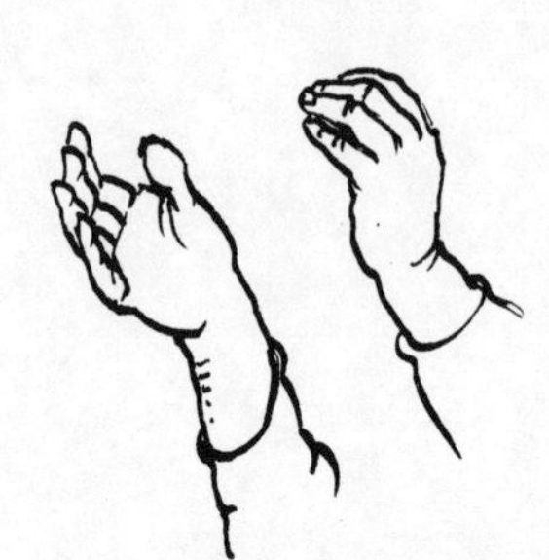

What to do
The children have to listen to a list of rhyming words and clap when they hear the odd one out, eg fat, cat, mat, log (clap), rat. You can either deliver the words live or pre-record them on cassette and play them back to the class.

Once the children have mastered this stage, the game can be varied by asking them to clap when they hear the word which rhymes with the first one in the list, eg pen, paw, tea, ten (clap).

Rhyming things

Age range
Five to seven.

Group size
Small group, ie five or six children.

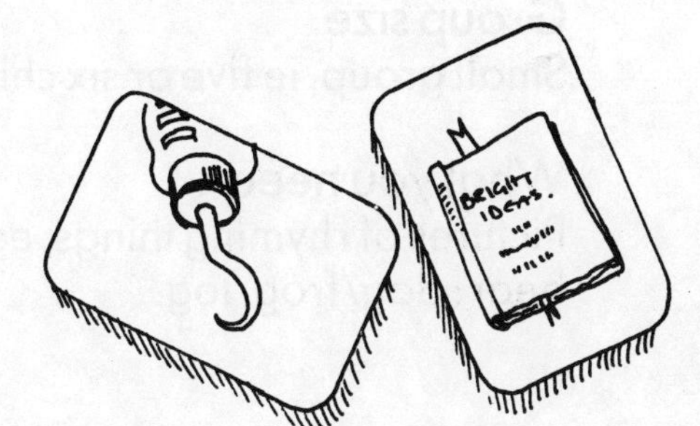

What you need
Pairs of objects (or pictures of objects) which rhyme, eg ring/string; cat/hat; mice/dice; brick/stick; book/hook; mug/rug.

What to do
Spread the objects (or the pictures) on a table and ask the children to help you to find the rhyming pairs. Pick up one object, say its name and ask one of the children to find the object whose name rhymes with it.

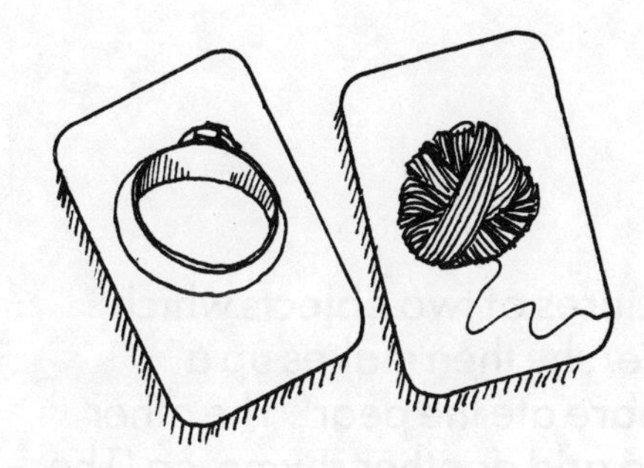

Add a rhyme

Age range
Five to seven.

Group size
Small group, ie five or six children.

What you need
Pictures of rhyming things, eg man/van/fan; pear/hare/bear; dog/frog/log.

What to do
Ask one child to pick out pictures of two objects which rhyme, eg pear and hare. He/she then makes up a sentence about them, 'The hare ate the pear'. The other children then take it in turn to add another rhyme, eg 'The hare ate the pear at the fair', or 'The hare ate the pear over there'.

What's missing?

Age range
Five to nine.

Group size
Small group, ie five to eight children.

What you need
A collection of pictures of objects which rhyme, eg gun/bun; hat/rat; nail/pail; coat/goat; man/fan; egg/peg; car/star; pen/hen; mug/jug; flag/stag. The important thing is that each rhyme should be different.

What to do
Make sure that the children can name the objects and work out the rhyming pair. Then spread out the cards on a table, send one of the children out of the room (or ask him/her to close his/her eyes) and remove one or two of the cards. Whoever is 'it' then has to try to say which cards are missing. The answer can be worked out by a process of elimination, ie by matching up the rhyming pairs.

Follow-up
Older children may enjoy using the cards to play Pelmanism as on page 11.

Rhyming names

Age range
Five to seven.

Group size
Whole class.

What you need
No materials needed.

What to do
Often there is a rather dreary job to be done or instructions to be given to all the children in the class (eg clearing up after painting or asking children to line up in a certain order). The whole thing can be made more fun by trying to find rhymes for the children's names and seeing if they can guess whom you mean, eg Sally/alley; Tracey/racey; Joan/phone. The children will probably enjoy thinking up variations for themselves. (Try to make sure the children aren't given names which might upset them, eg Tony/bony.)

Follow-up
Once all the children have been given a rhyming nickname, put the names on tape and see if another class can guess to whom the names refer.

Have you heard the one about . . . ?

Age range
Five to eleven.

Group size
Small group, ie five or six children.

What you need
Tape-recorder and cassettes.

What to do
Jokes are yet another way of playing with language. Most children love them and have an endless supply of particular favourites. The class can take it in turns to record their jokes on tape, or share their jokes in small groups – again with each child taking it in turn to tell one.

Follow-up
The children might like to make a class joke tape to share with other classes.

What's wrong here?

Age range
Five to seven.

Group size
Small group, ie five or six children.

What you need
A book of nursery rhymes.

What to do
Explain to the children that you are going to tell them some nursery rhymes, but you are going to make some mistakes on purpose. Every time you make a mistake the children should clap and help you put it right, eg:

Little Bo Peep has lost her dog (sheep);

Jack and Jill went up the road (hill);

Mary, Mary quite bad-tempered (contrary),
How does your garden grow?

Wee Willie Winkie runs through the town,
Upstairs and downstairs in his pyjamas (nightgown);

Girls and boys come out to play,
The moon does shine as bright as summer (day).

Mary had a little lamb,
Its fleece was white as snow,
And everywhere that Mary went
The lamb was sure to come (go).

There was an old woman who lived in a shoe,
She had so many children she didn't know what to say (do).

Ding dong bell,
Pussy's in the river (well).

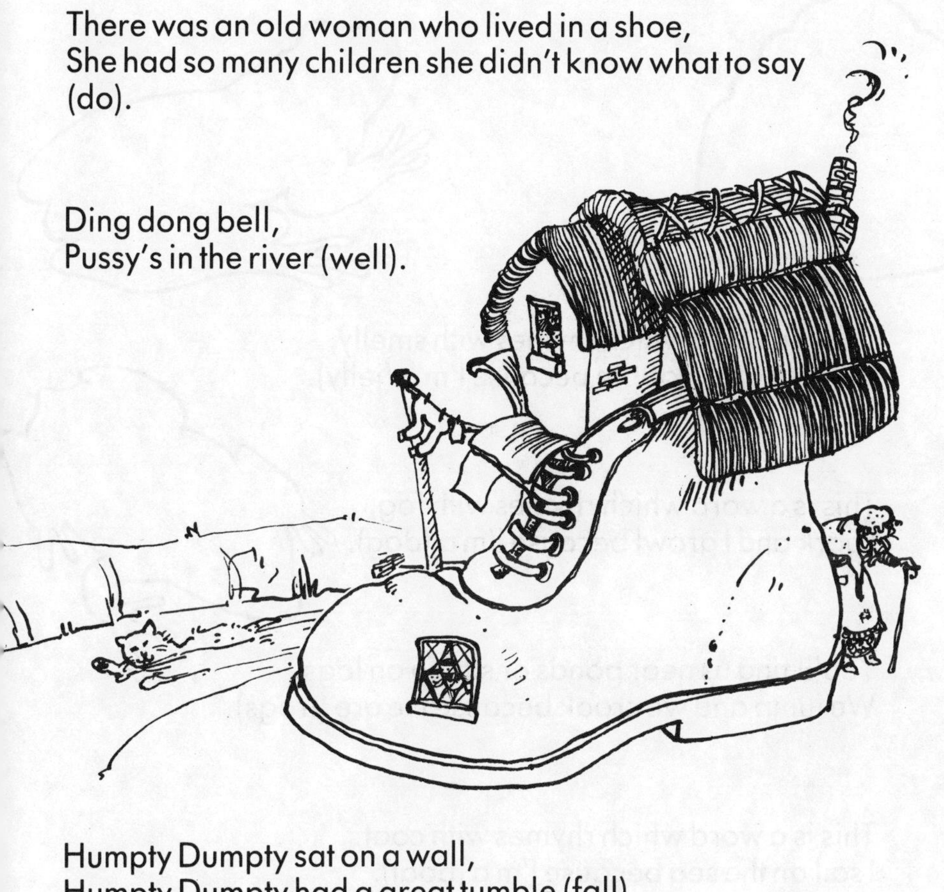

Humpty Dumpty sat on a wall,
Humpty Dumpty had a great tumble (fall).

Hey diddle diddle,
The cat and the trumpet (fiddle).

Georgie Porgie pudding and pie
Kissed the girls and made them laugh (cry).

I had a little nut tree, nothing would it bear
But a silver nutmeg and a golden apple (pear).

Tom, Tom the piper's son
Stole a pig and away did creep (run).

Riddles

Age range
Five to eleven.

Group size
Whole class.

What you need
A supply of home-made riddles; alternatively, you can use these , either delivered live or pre-recorded on tape.

What to do
Once the children have grasped the idea of rhymes, they usually enjoy riddles where the rhyme is an extra clue:

This is a word which rhymes with bun,
You feel warm when I shine because I'm the (sun).

This is a word which rhymes with bake,
I'm delicious to eat because I'm a (cake).

This is a word which rhymes with smelly,
I wibble and wobble because I'm a (jelly).

This is a word which rhymes with fog,
I bark and I growl because I'm a (dog).

You'll find us near ponds or sitting on logs,
We jump and we croak because we are (frogs).

This is a word which rhymes with coat,
I sail on the sea because I'm a (boat).

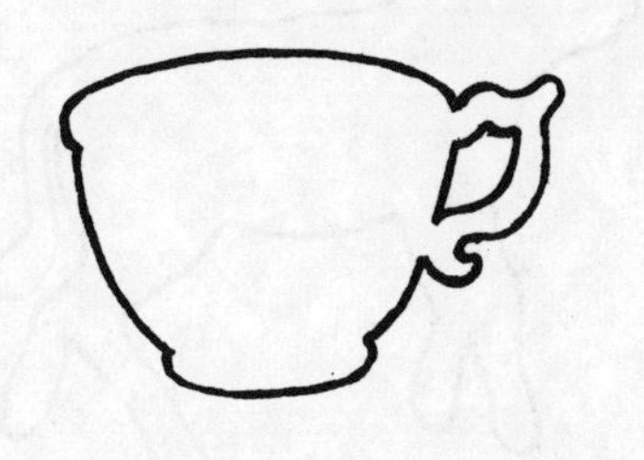

This is a word which rhymes with up,
You can drink out of me because I'm a (cup).

This is a word which rhymes with meat,
You use me for walking because I'm your (feet).

This is a word which rhymes with pear,
I grow on your head because I'm your (hair).

This is a word which rhymes with spoon,
I shine brightly at night because I'm the (moon).

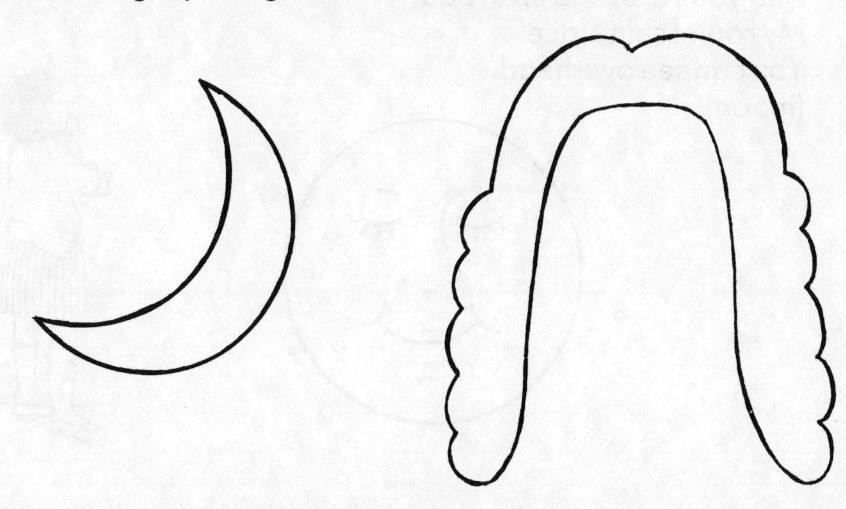

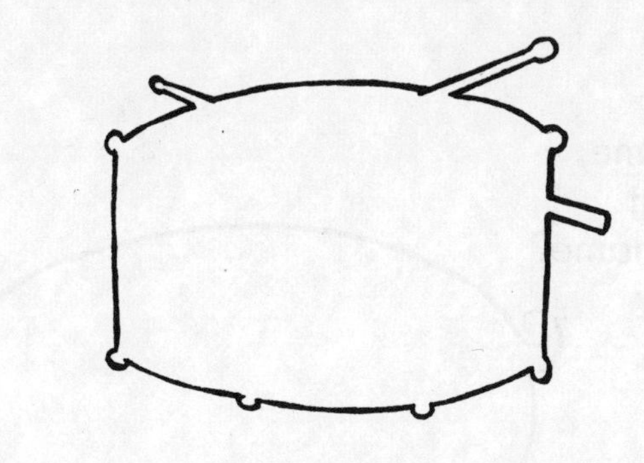

When you bang me hard I go rumpa-tum-tum,
I'm played in a band because I'm a (drum).

This is a word which rhymes with toes,
You use me to smell with because I'm your (nose).

I'm useful for journeys when you're going far,
But I need lots of petrol because I'm a (car).

This is a word which rhymes with cat,
It goes on your head because it's a (hat).

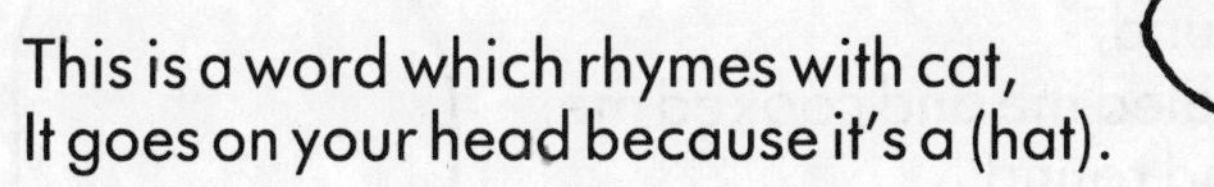

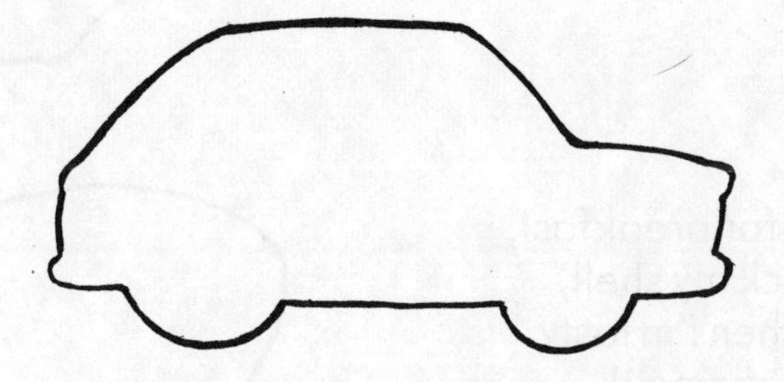

I live in a sty,
I grunt and I'm tame,
You like me to eat
Now what is my name?
(pig)

I mend your clothes,
I'm sharp and I'm bright,
I've only one eye
And that has no sight.
(needle)

I'm brown and I'm hard,
I grow in the ground,
When you've peeled me and cooked me,
I'm soft, white and round.
(potato)

You eat me for breakfast,
But first crack my shell,
If I'm fresh then I'm tasty,
If not – what a smell!
(egg)

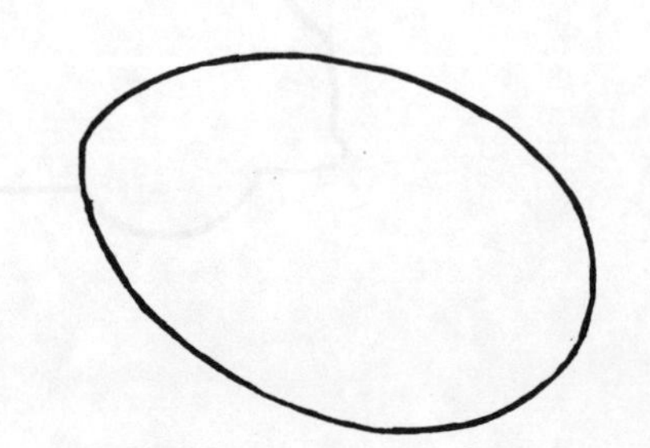

I'm only a baby,
I'm covered with wool,
My mother's a sheep,
Mary took me to school.
(lamb)

You've two of your own
On each side of your head,
You use them to listen
And hear what is said.
(ears)

When the stars are bright
And you're tucked up in bed,
My round shiny face
You can see overhead.
(moon)

I'm a pet that you love,
I'm furry and tame,
I love fish and milk,
Can you guess my name?
(cat)

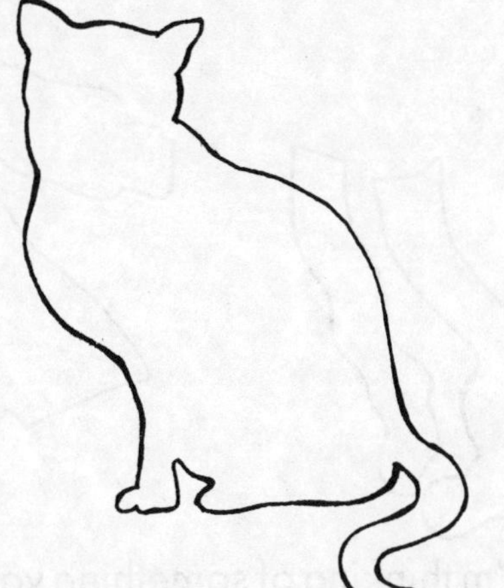

Now here's a cheerful colour,
The colour of the sun,
Of daffodils and butter,
Who can guess it? Everyone!
(yellow)

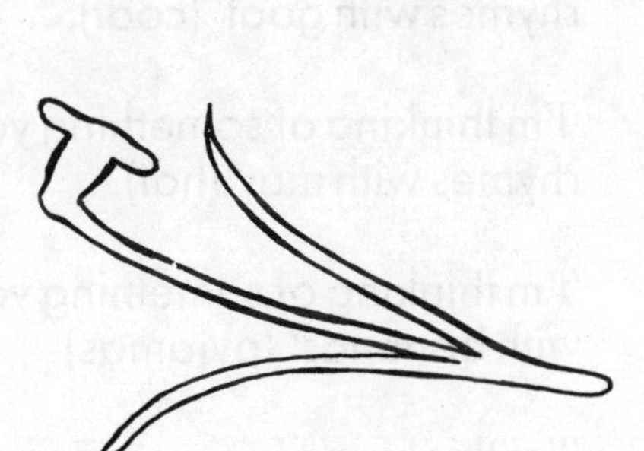

I grow on a tree,
Squirrels love me and hide
Me away, I've a shell,
But I'm crunchy inside.
(nut)

You put me up
When the rain's beating down,
And I'm just as useful
In country or town.
(umbrella)

I'm a big animal
That you see at the zoo,
I've a very nice trunk
I can squirt water through.
(elephant)

I'm a bright little bird
With some red on my chest,
If you dig up some worms
They're the food I like best.
(robin)

You cook things inside me,
But when you open my door
Out comes all the heat,
So close me for sure.
(oven or cooker)

Follow-up

The children may like to invent and tape their own riddles. It doesn't matter if their versions don't scan – the important thing at this stage is the rhyme.

I'm thinking of something to wear

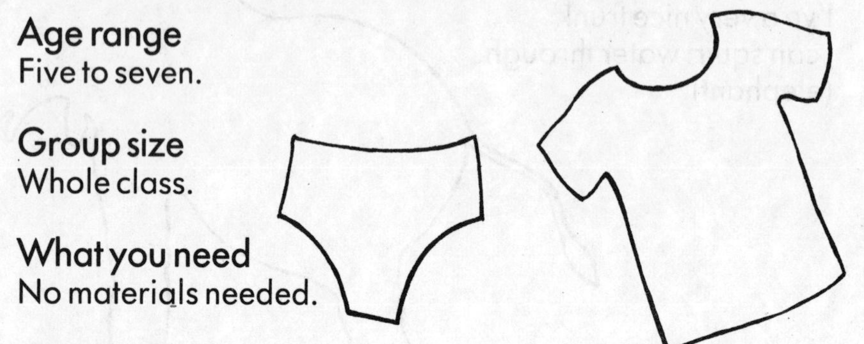

Age range
Five to seven.

Group size
Whole class.

What you need
No materials needed.

What to do
The children have to guess which article of clothing you are thinking of, using the rhyme as a clue, eg:

'I'm thinking of something you wear on your feet which rhymes with hoots' (boots).

'I'm thinking of something you wear on your legs which rhymes with fights' (tights).

'I'm thinking of something you wear when it's cold which rhymes with goat' (coat).

'I'm thinking of something you wear on your head which rhymes with mat' (hat).

'I'm thinking of something you wear in bed which rhymes with bananas' (pyjamas).

'I'm thinking of something you wear round your neck which rhymes with laugh' (scarf). (Regional pronunciation variation.)

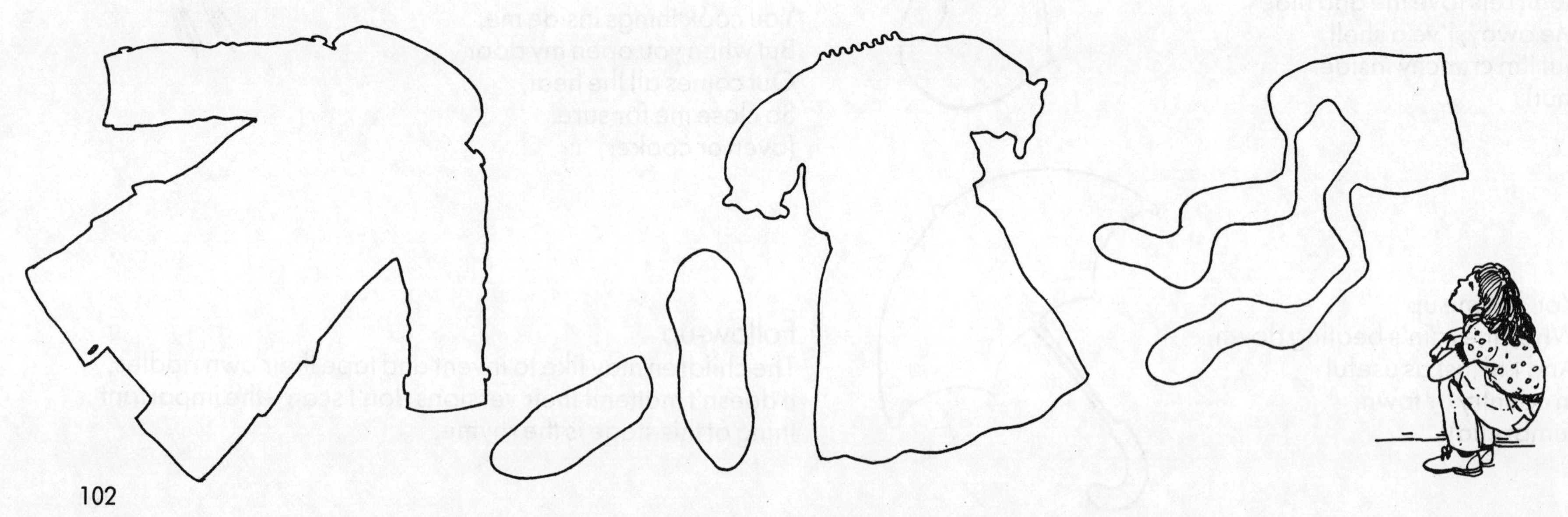

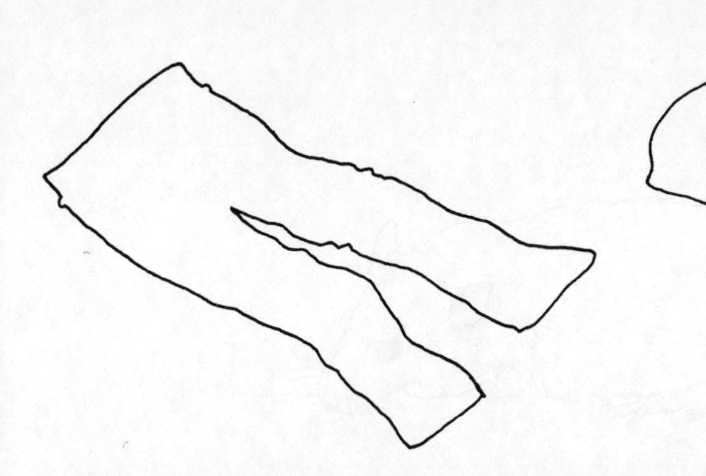

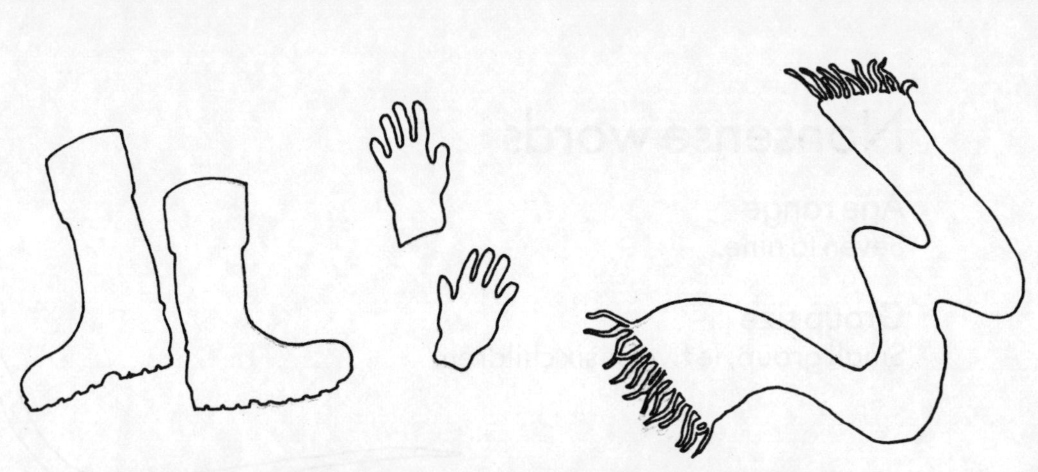

''I'm thinking of something you wear on your legs which rhymes with beans' (jeans).

'I'm thinking of something you wear under your sweater which rhymes with best' (vest).

'I'm thinking of something you wear on your hands which rhymes with doves' (gloves).

'I'm thinking of something you wear on your feet which rhymes with bruise' (shoes).

'I'm thinking of something you wear on your feet which rhymes with handles' (sandals).

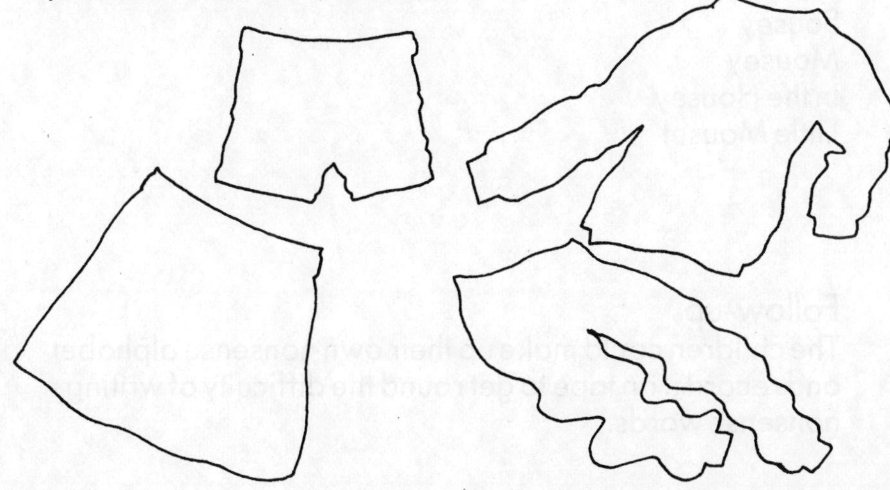

'I'm thinking of something you wear when it's hot which rhymes with warts' (shorts).

'I'm thinking of something you wear under your trousers which rhymes with ants' (pants).

'I'm thinking of something you tuck in your trousers which rhymes with hurt' (shirt).

'I'm thinking of something girls wear which rhymes with press' (dress).

'I'm thinking of something girls wear which rhymes with dirt' (skirt).

'I'm thinking of something you wear on your feet which rhymes with box' (socks).

Follow-up

The children might like to make up their own riddles – perhaps, 'I'm thinking of something to eat' – and record them to play to another class.

Nonsense words

Age range
Seven to nine.

Group size
Small group, ie five or six children.

What you need
No materials essential but Edward Lear's *Nonsense Alphabet* is a good starting point.

What to do
The idea in this game is for the children to parrot the nonsense rhymes and words you tell them. You may use any nonsense material of your own, or the dips, rhymes and jingles in this book, or some of Lear's *Nonsense Alphabet*, eg:

M was once a little mouse,
Mousey
Bousey
Sousey
Mousey
In the Housey
Little Mouse!

Follow-up
The children could make up their own nonsense alphabet and record it on tape to get round the difficulty of writing nonsense words.

Tongue-twisters

Age range
Seven to nine.

Group size
Small group, ie five or six children.

What you need
A tape-recorder.

What to do
Ask the children to think of as many tongue-twisters as they can – perhaps parents, grandparents and other relatives can supply a few. Once there is a good selection – either recorded on tape or written down – the children could practise a favourite and then try to make a tape of really well-delivered tongue-twisters. Different groups might even like to have a tongue-twister competition. Here are a few old favourites:

Red leather, yellow leather.

She sells sea shells by the sea-shore.

Sister Susie's sewing shirts for sailors.

Peter Piper picked a peck of pickled peppers.

Nonsense animals

Age range
Seven to eleven.

Group size
Whole class or any size group.

What you need
No materials essential but pictures/models of zoo and farm animals may help.

What to do
The aim of the game is to invent a new animal which is a mixture of two or more familiar ones. Spike Milligan's 'Hipporhinostricow' or James Reeves' *Prefabulous Animiles* can be useful starters.

Several children can then shut their eyes, pick out several animals at random and try to invent a name for the animal which would result from a combination of them. They could then go on to discuss what such an animal would be able to do.

Nonsense alphabet zoo

Age range
Seven to eleven.

Group size
Whole class.

What you need
Shoe boxes without lids, cardboard, glue, paints/crayons and string.

What to do
The children try to invent imaginary zoo animals. James Reeves' *Prefabulous Animiles* and *More Prefabulous Animiles*, and Spike Milligan's 'Hipporhinostricow' and *Zoophabets* are all useful starters.

At first, it may help to restrict the children to animals beginning with just a few consonants. Once the children have decided on a name, they can then draw or paint their animals and put them into shoe-box cages with string bars. When it's feeding time, the children can choose appropriate food for the animals – for example, a tibble might eat trousers, tights, toast, telegraph poles, telephones and tractors; a quango might eat quoits, queens, quavers.

Follow-up
The children could gradually build up and display a whole alphabet zoo.

REPRODUCIBLE MATERIAL

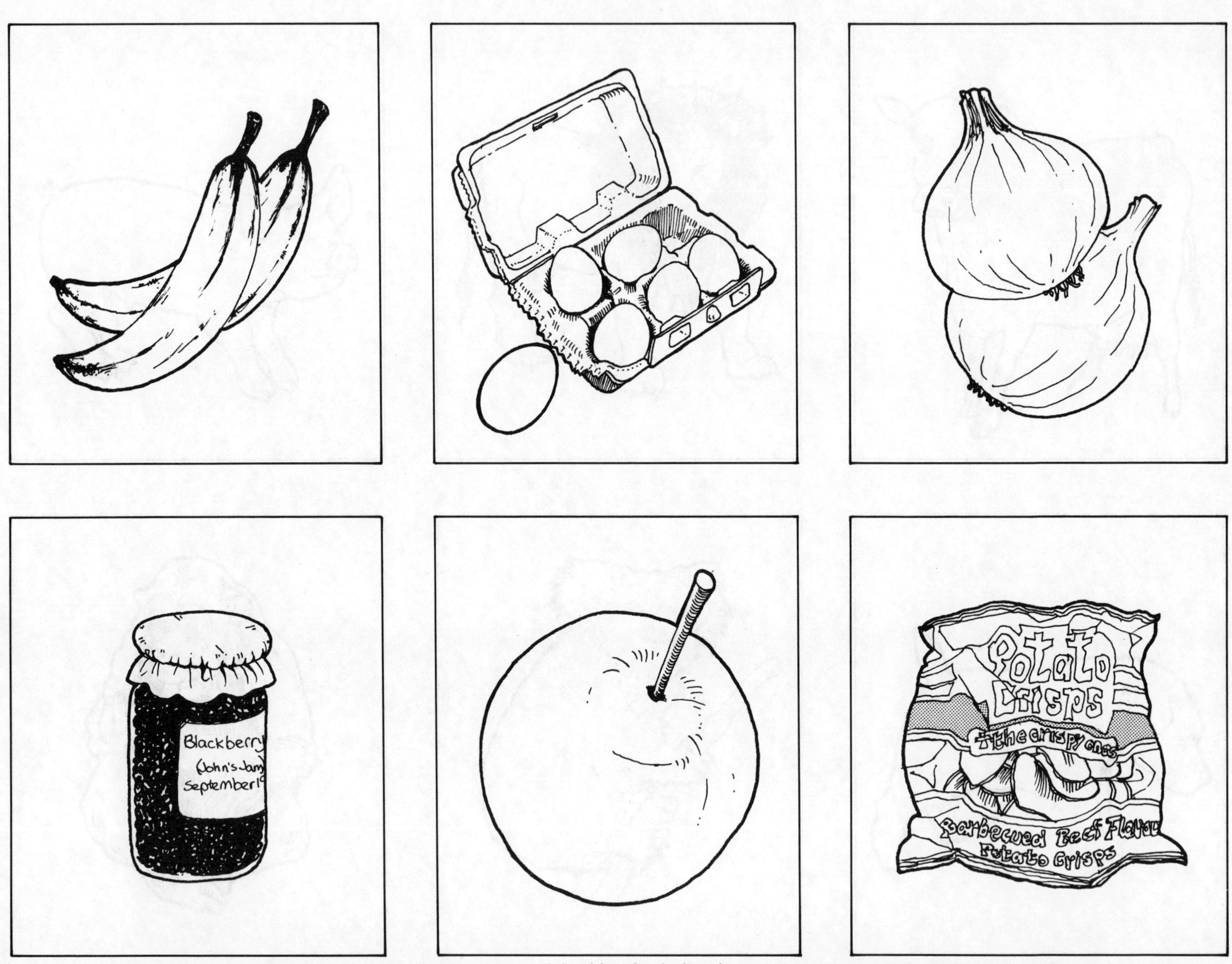
Blackberry
Potato Crisps
the crispy ones
Potato Crisps

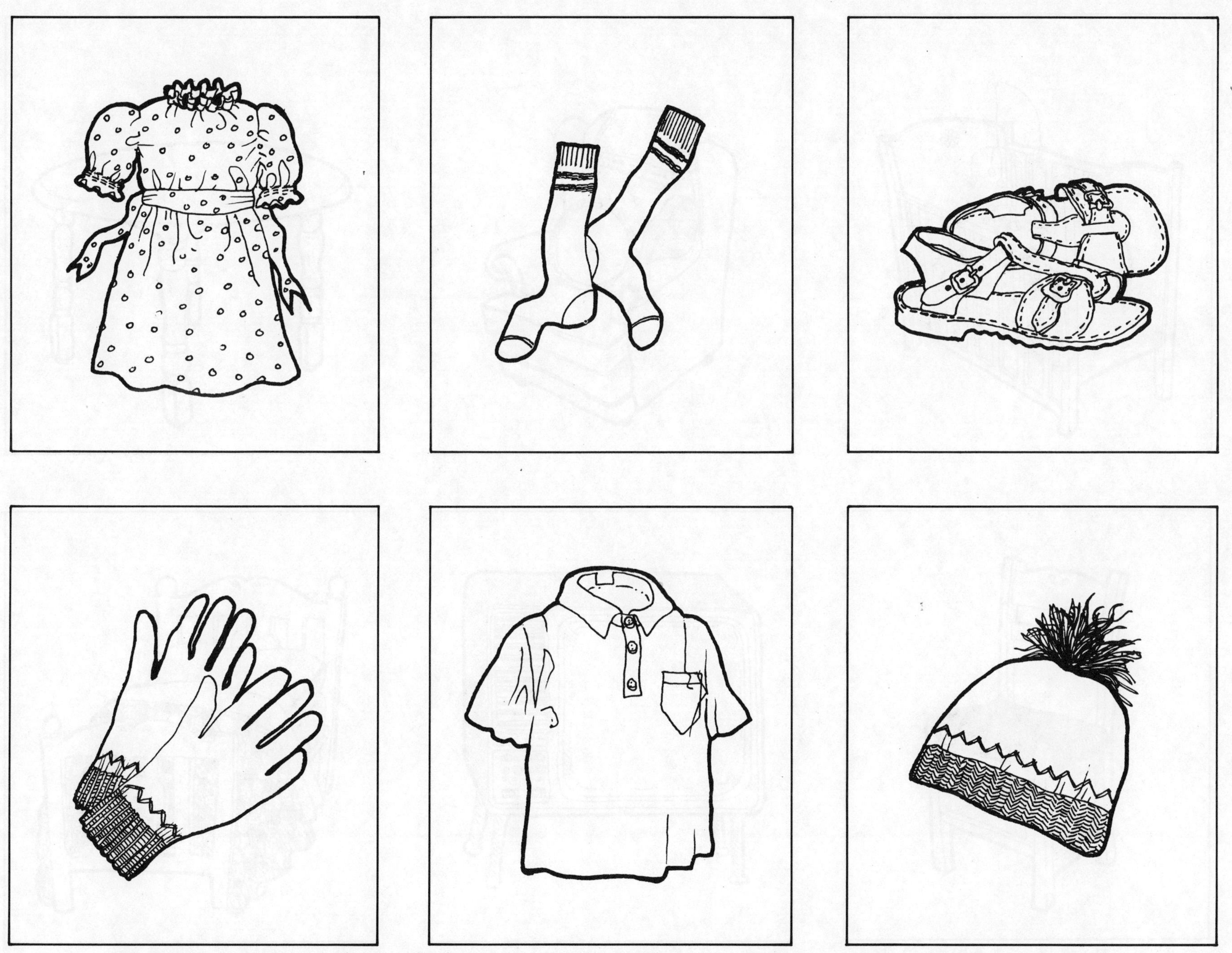

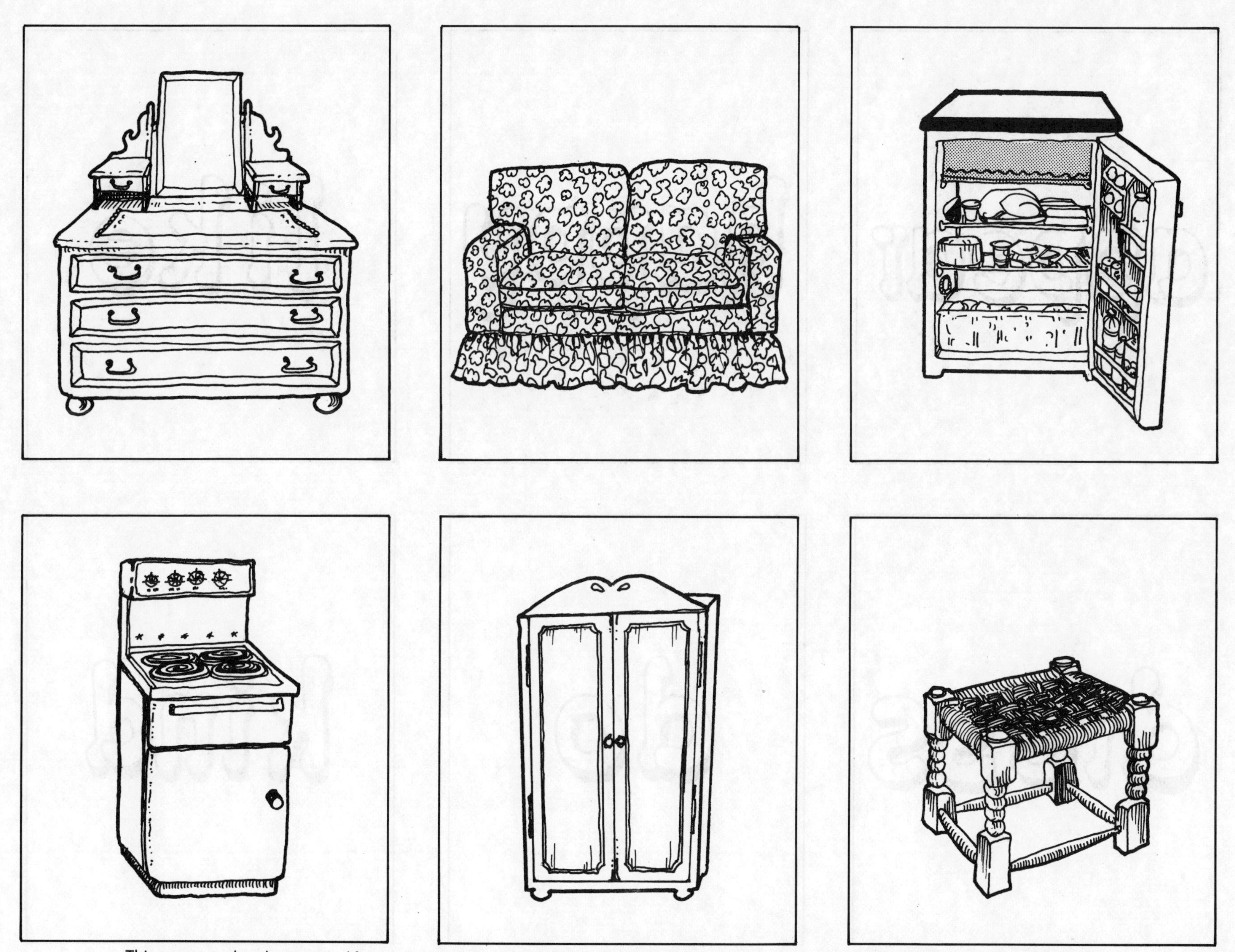

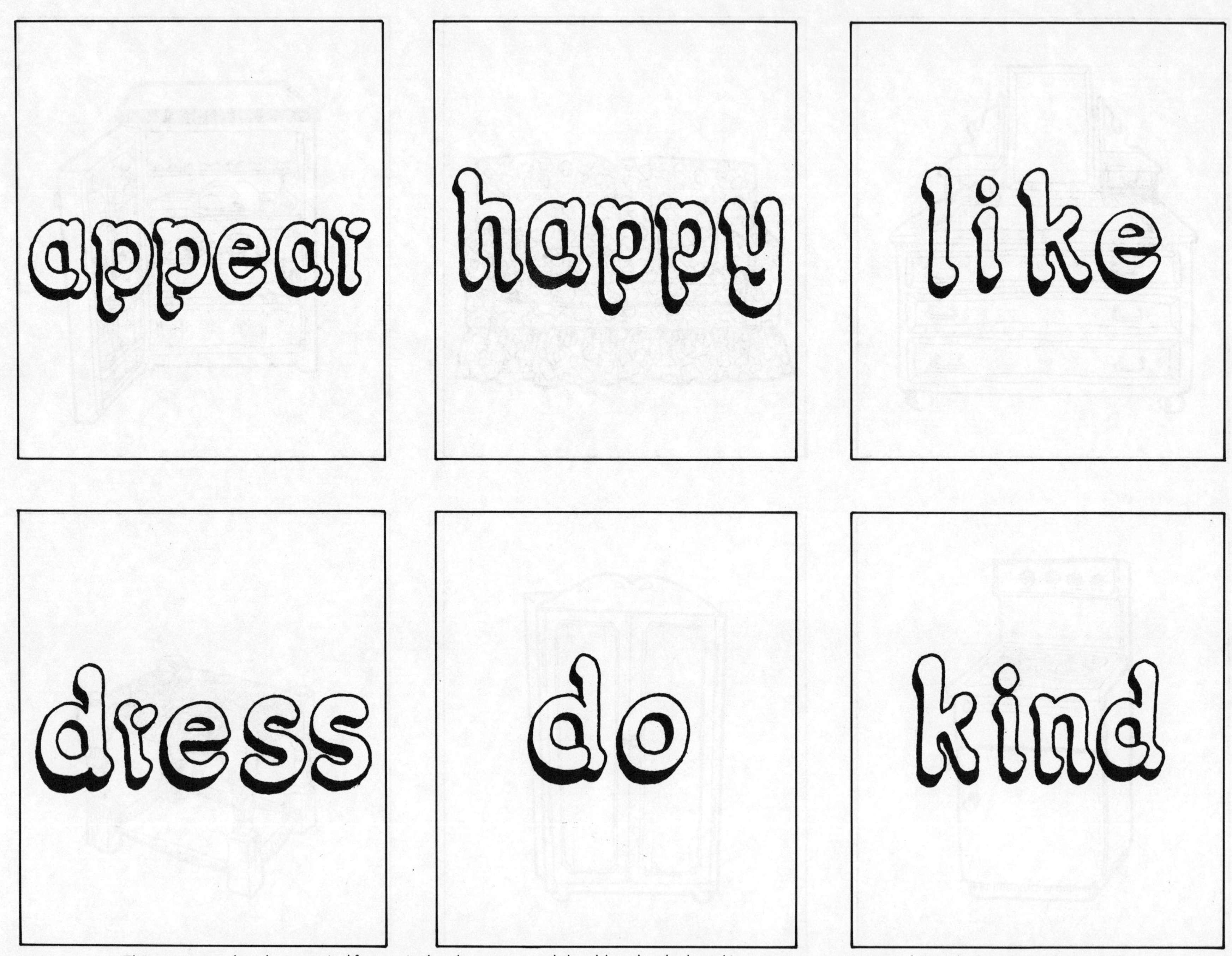
appear
happy
like
dress
do
kind

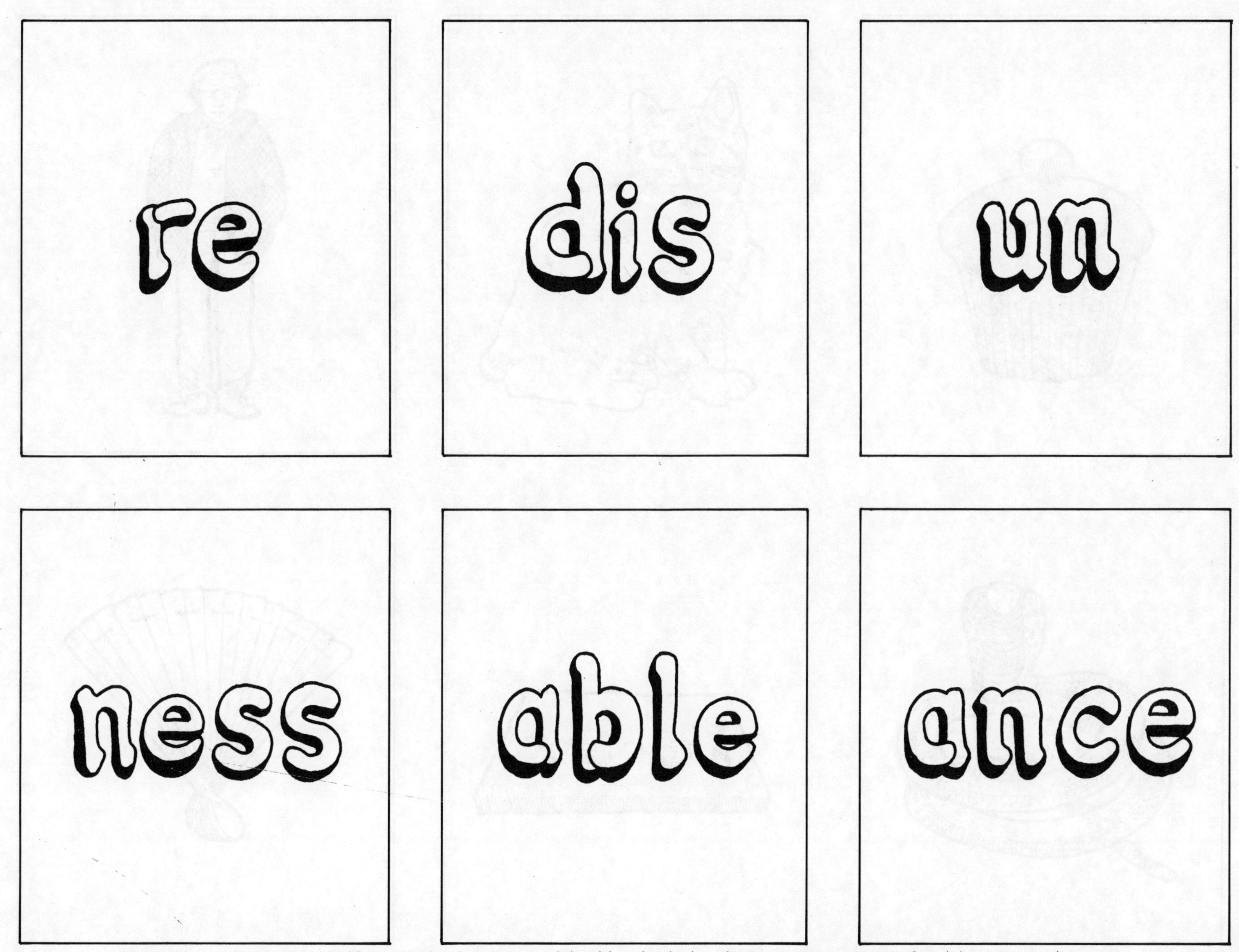
re
dis
un
ness
able
ance

Welcome

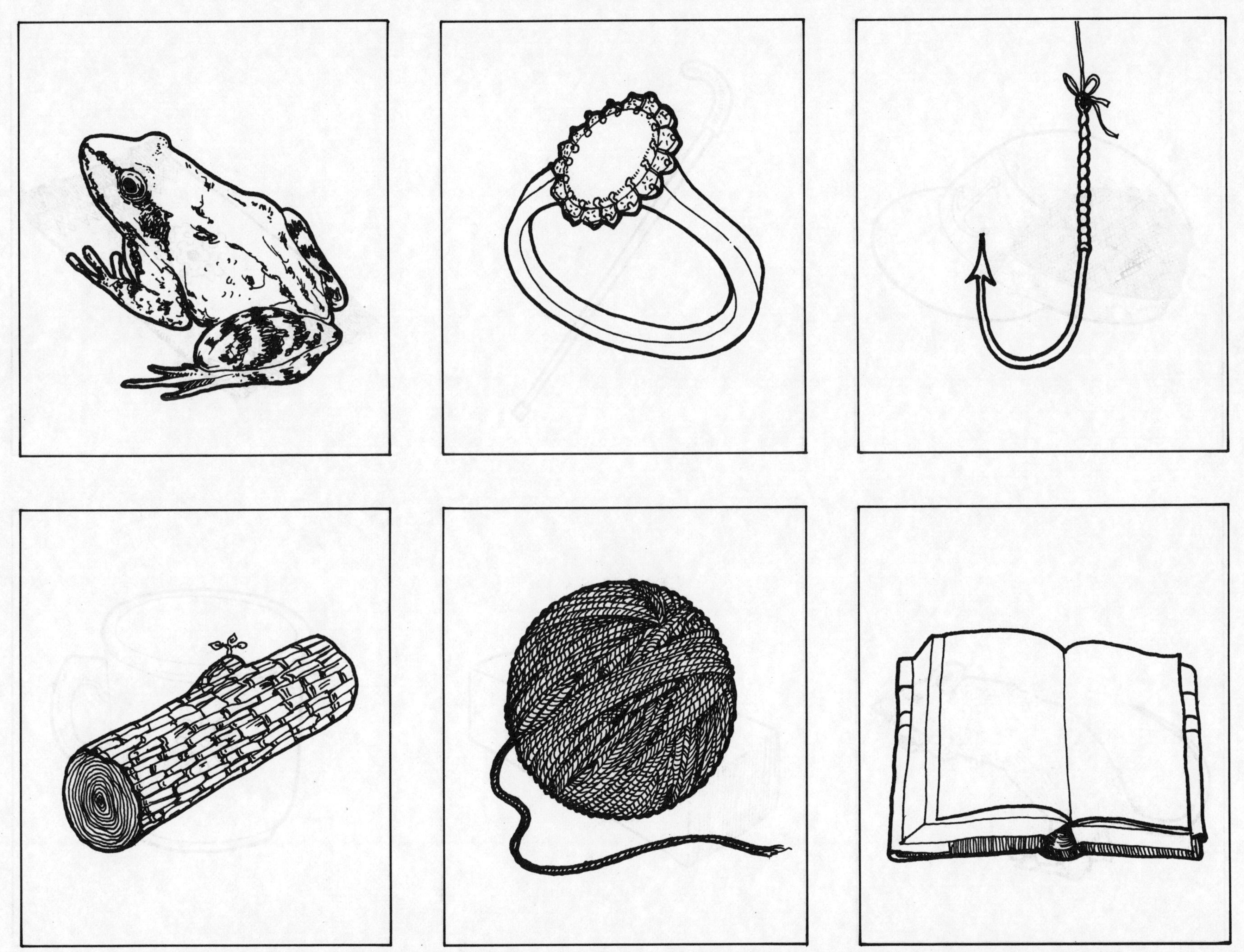

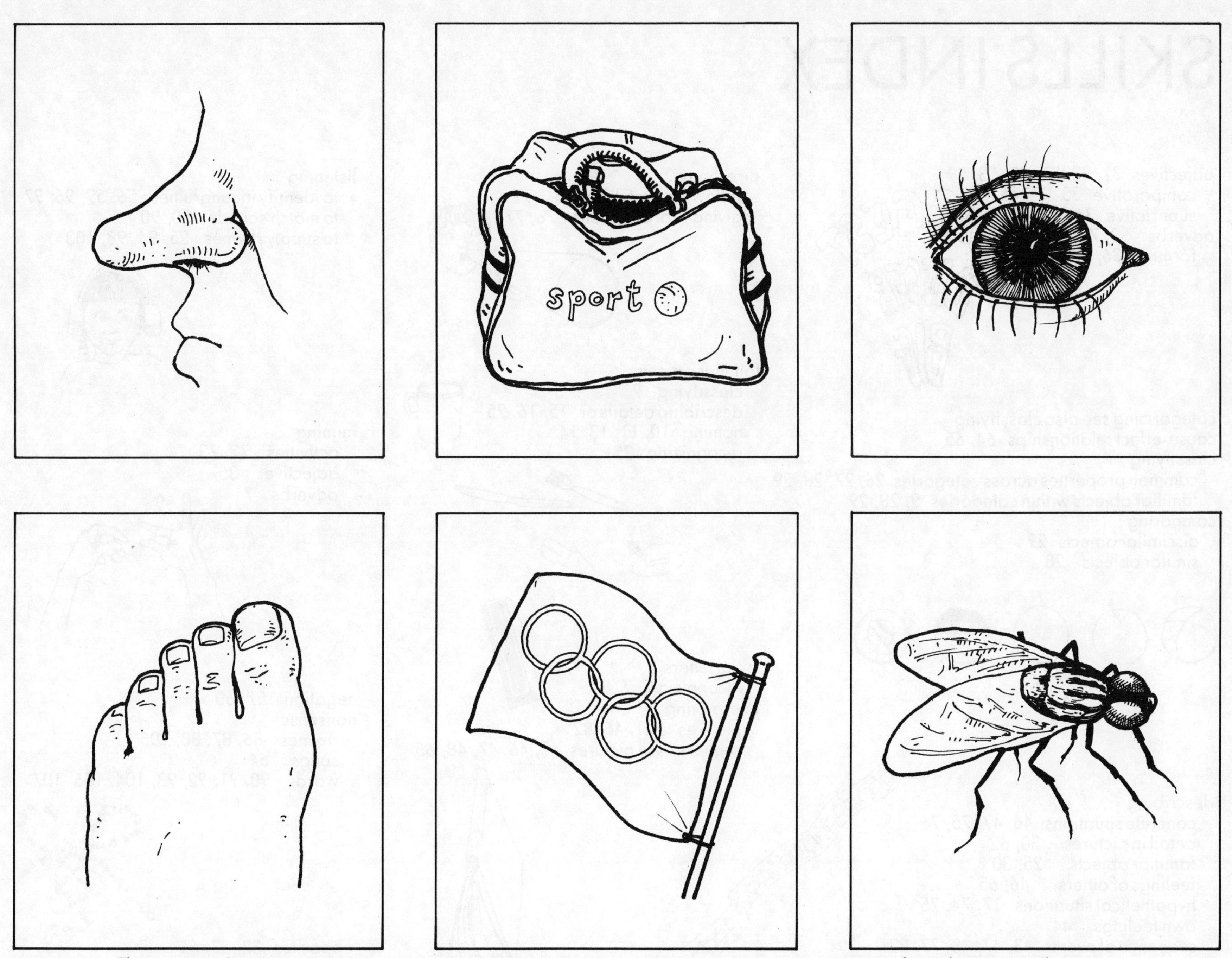
sport

SKILLS INDEX

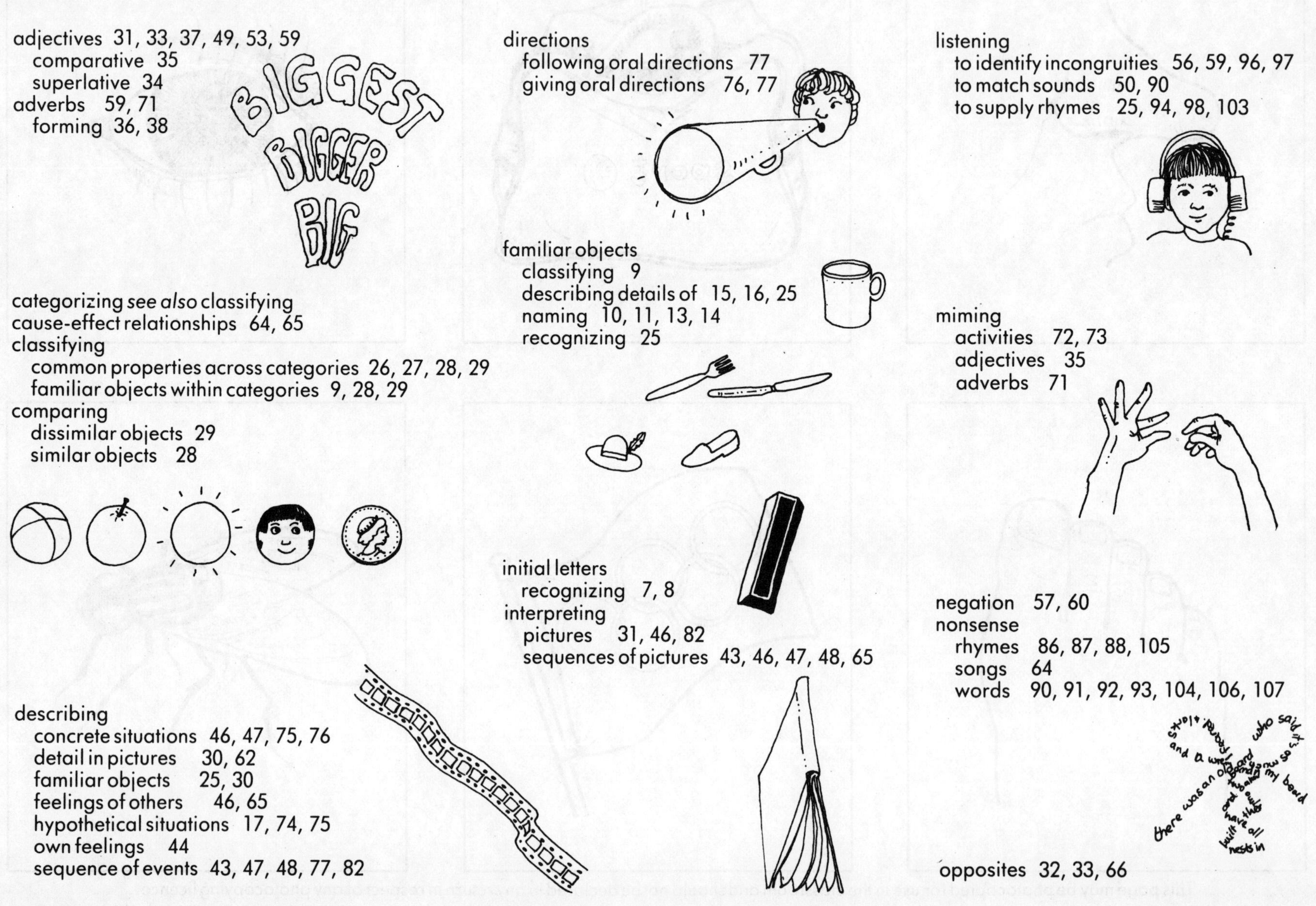

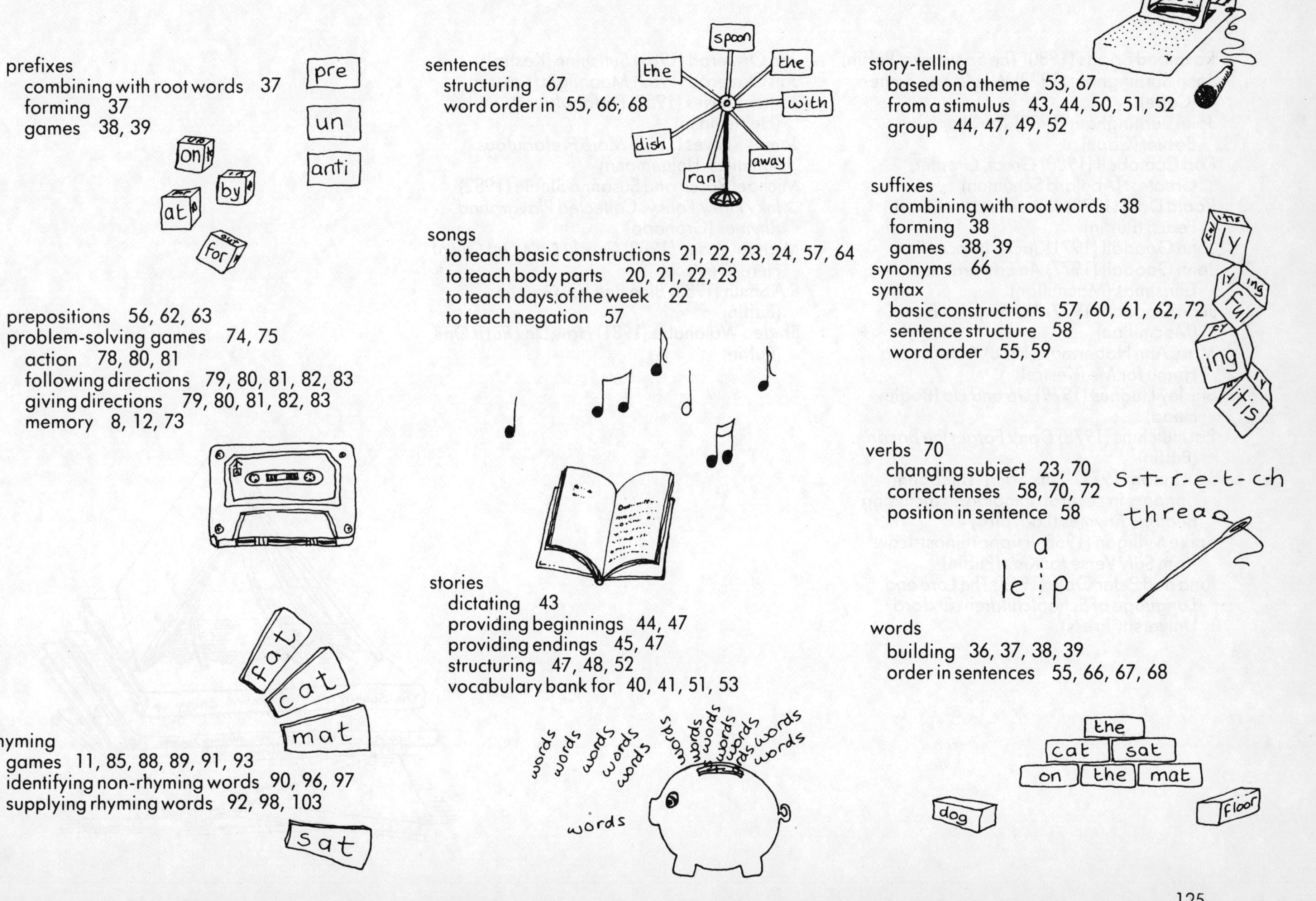
pre
un
anti
on
by
at
for
spoon
the
the
with
dish
away
ran
fat
cat
mat
sat
words
S-t-r-e-t-c-h
thread
le a p
ly
ful
ing
itis
the
cat sat
on the mat
dog
floor

REFERENCES

Raymond Briggs (1980) *The Snowman* (Puffin)

John Burningham (1978) *Would You Rather* (Cape)

John Burningham (1980) *The Shopping Basket* (Cape)

Rod Campbell (1980) *Great, Greater, Greatest* (Abelard Schuman)

Roald Dahl (1973) *James and the Giant Peach* (Puffin)

John Goodall (1971) *Jacko* (Macmillan)

John Goodall (1977) *An Edwardian Christmas* (Macmillan)

John Goodall (1977) *The Surprise Picnic* (Macmillan)

Mary Ann Hoberman (1978) *A House is a Home for Me* (Kestrel)

Shirley Hughes (1979) *Up and Up* (Bodley Head)

Pat Hutchins (1978) *Don't Forget the Bacon* (Puffin)

J A Lindon (1977) 'Sink Song' This poem appears in several anthologies including *Bedtime Rhymes* (Ladybird)

Spike Milligan (1968) 'Hipporhinostricow' from *Silly Verse for Kids* (Puffin)

Iona and Peter Opie (1967) *The Lore and Language of Schoolchildren* (Oxford University Press)

Jan Ormerod (1981) *Sunshine* (Kestrel)

Jan Ormerod (1982) *Moonlight* (Kestrel)

James Reeves (1957) *Prefabulous Animiles* (Heinemann)

James Reeves (1975) *More Prefabulous Animiles* (Heinemann)

Michael Rosen and Susanna Steele (1982) *Inky Pinky Ponky: Collected Playground Rhymes* (Granada)

Michael Rosen (1983) *Quick, Let's Get Out of Here* (Deutsch)

R A Smith (1983) *Blue Bell Hill Games* (Puffin)

Shigeo Watanabe (1981) *How Do I Put It On?* (Puffin)

ACKNOWLEDGEMENTS

The editors and publishers extend grateful thanks for reuse of material first published in *Child Education* to: Mollie Bradford for 'Whisk up a song'; Vivienne Catton and Cecile Stevenson for 'Those Bones', 'This is the way we do it' and 'I went to the chemist and I bought'; Sylvia Collicott for 'The treasure box'; Paul Cornwell for 'What would you do if?'; Gabriel Maunder for 'Telling a story'.

Every effort has been made to trace and acknowledge contributors. If any right has been omitted, the publishers offer their apologies and will rectify this in subsequent editions following notification.

I would also like to thank George, Nicky and Layla for their contributions to the dips and skipping rhymes and, in particular, Sue Quilliam for her much appreciated help and encouragement.